A Survey
of
New Testament History

Jonathan Turner

80CB

ೞೲೞ

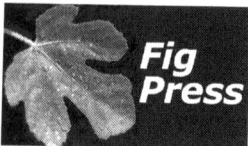

Fig
Press

Table of Contents

ഓ‍ോ

List of Illustrations

80C3

In the Fullness of Time

Introduction: Why do a survey of New Testament history?

One of the best things a congregation can do to promote spiritual growth is emphasize expository speaking and teaching – going verse by verse through some book of the Bible. This is appropriate for, as Paul writes, the Scriptures can make us wise for salvation (2 Timothy 3:15). In the same passage Paul goes on to say, "All Scripture is God-breathed and is useful for teaching, rebuking, correcting and training in righteousness, so that the man of God may be thoroughly equipped for every good work." (2 Timothy 3:16-17 NIV) So, it is essential that we spend time studying, assimilating and applying the Scriptures to our lives.

Having said that, it is possible to concentrate so much on the detail that we miss the big picture. To put it another way, we cannot really understand the detail unless we first have an understanding of the context and framework of what we're looking at. How does a particular incident, how does a particular book or letter fit into God's over-all plan? These studies provide a look at the broad picture. I intend them to provide you with the background and context to help you understand how the New Testament fits together.

I.   The Focus Is Christ

Part of the 'big picture' is understanding what the point of the Bible is. We have a natural tendency to be selfish. Unfortunately, this tendency comes to the fore even when we study the Bible. It's very tempting to concentrate on God's promises to us. We ask ourselves the question – and it is a very legitimate question – "How does this benefit me?" It's true that we need to know how Scripture affects us. We need the hope that meditating on God's promises gives us. But, even while thinking about our relationship to God and how Scripture applies to us, it is possible to miss the point. We will never arrive at a proper understanding of Scripture and what God is doing in history until we realize that the focus of the entire Bible is Jesus Christ. It is not about us, per se. It is not really even about our relationship with God, per se. This was the fundamental mistake which the Jews of

Jesus' day made in regard to the Scriptures: They missed what they are all about. Jesus said, "You diligently study the Scriptures because you think that by them you possess eternal life. These are the Scriptures that testify about me, yet you refuse to come to me to have life." (John 5:39-40 NIV)

How, then, should we approach the Bible? Since the focus of all Scripture is Christ, we must study the Bible with the same focus or we will never arrive at a proper understanding of it. God's purpose is to make us like Christ. For example, Paul defines spiritual maturity as "...attaining to the whole measure of the fullness of Christ." (Ephesians 4:13 NIV)

It is not God's purpose to make us happy, but to make us like Jesus. It is not His purpose to make us better people, but to make us like Jesus. Happiness and a better character are not end results to be desired in themselves. They are byproducts of something far more important and fundamental, that is, becoming like Christ. Our focus should not be on the things promised so much as on becoming Christlike which makes obtaining the promises possible. When trying to apply Scripture we should not ask how we will benefit so much as how applying it can make us more like Jesus.

II.   Setting The Stage

The New Testament didn't appear out of a vacuum. Over a period of thousands of years, God very carefully set the stage for the coming of Christ and the spreading of the Gospel message.

The first glimpse of God's plan of redemption came right after Adam and Eve sinned in the Garden of Eden. God promised that someday an offspring of the woman would crush Satan's head (Genesis 3:15).

After Adam and Eve sinned, mankind became more and more corrupt until God had to destroy the entire world in a flood except for Noah and his family. Noah's ark is a powerful picture of the salvation which God was going to offer the world through Jesus Christ.

After the flood, mankind spread over all the earth and divided into peoples and tribes. Out of all of them God picked one man through whom to start to reveal His will. From Abraham's descendants, God picked one son. From that son's descendants God picked another son through whom He built a nation, set apart in order to fulfill the divine plan.

> **Tangent:** Why did God pick the Jewish people through whom to fulfill salvation history? We don't know. Scripture does not tell us all the reasons. However, the Jewish people have one virtue that sets them apart from all other peoples and may be why God chose them. This is speculation, but it seems that the Jewish people were the only ones who preserved God's word. Think about it. Only eight people survived the flood. They all knew what had happened. They all knew what God said to Noah. They all knew the promises. Yet only one branch of the family chose to preserve the record. Only one branch of the family preserved a knowledge of God. All the rest turned away from God into idolatry and garbled the history of what happened. Though the Jewish people had plenty of problems themselves; though they were often unfaithful, they still preserved the Word. I think it was for this reason that God chose them as the people through whom to bring the Savior into the world.

Throughout the Old Testament period, God continued the winnowing process. Out of the nation, He selected one tribe. Out of the tribe, He picked one family and one lineage until last of all, His choice fell on one, probably teen-aged, girl in Nazareth in Galilee.

In addition to winnowing out the lineage, and eventually the person through whom the Savior would be brought into the world, there were some other really important things which God did during the Old Testament period.

> 1) God taught mankind some key spiritual concepts and ideas and developed the vocabulary necessary to express them. It's very difficult to communicate with someone unless you speak the same language. It's very difficult to lead someone to new truth unless that truth is an extension or expression of

concepts already understood. It's this way in any area of human experience. For example, it's impossible to learn to read unless you first learn the alphabet and the sounds letters make. In the same way, each area of life and each skill has it's own vocabulary.

The same is true in the spiritual realm. In order to be reconciled to God or even understand the divine plan, mankind needed to learn some key concepts and vocabulary. Through the centuries, God patiently taught about such things as sin, holiness, sacrifice, covenant, mercy, justice, propitiation, mediation and justification. This was one of the functions of the Mosaic Law. For example, Paul writes, "...I would not have known what sin was except through the law. For I would not have known what coveting really was if the law had not said, "Do not covet."" (Romans 7:7 NIV)

2) Mankind learned that it needed a Savior. One of the constants in human nature is the notion that we can save ourselves. We think that we can be good enough. We can earn our way into God's good graces. Through God's dealings with the Israelites, it became abundantly clear that nobody is capable of living up to His standards of perfection. No one was able to keep God's Law. Rules and regulations cannot save. Salvation and reconciliation with God must be based on a different principle.

3) God prepared the world to receive the Savior. Sending the Savior into the world was not a random event. God waited until conditions were right. He was working through history to shape the world so that the Gospel message could spread rapidly to many different peoples in a short amount of time. Paul writes, "...when we were children, we were in slavery under the basic principles of the world. But when the time had fully come, God sent his Son, born of a woman, born under law, to redeem those under law, that we might receive the full rights of sons." (Galatians 4:3-5 NIV)

III.   400 Years Of Silence?

Let's explore this last point a little more. The constant message of the Old Testament was that a Savior is coming. Prophet after prophet directed people's attention to the promise that one day God would redeem His people. The big question was, when? Peter writes, "Concerning this salvation, the prophets, who spoke of the grace that was to come to you, searched intently and with the greatest care, trying to find out the time and circumstances to which the Spirit of Christ in them was pointing when he predicted the sufferings of Christ and the glories that would follow." (1 Peter 1:10-11 NIV)

The last prophet to write was Malachi. He closed his book with a prophecy that the day of the Lord was coming (Malachi 4:5).

When we look back in time, we tend to telescope history. When we read the pages of the Old Testament, it's easy to think of the events happening right after each other without realizing the long stretches of time that come between them. There must have been many times when it seemed that God was not working and that He was never going to fulfill the promise of sending a Savior. This was the situation after Malachi wrote. God spoke to Malachi and, then, fell silent. There were no more prophecies for 400 years.

But was God really silent? No! For those who were listening and watching, God's work was plain to see. God had revealed a precise road-map and timetable of events through the prophet Daniel, leading up to the coming of the Savior. Let's take a brief look at it.

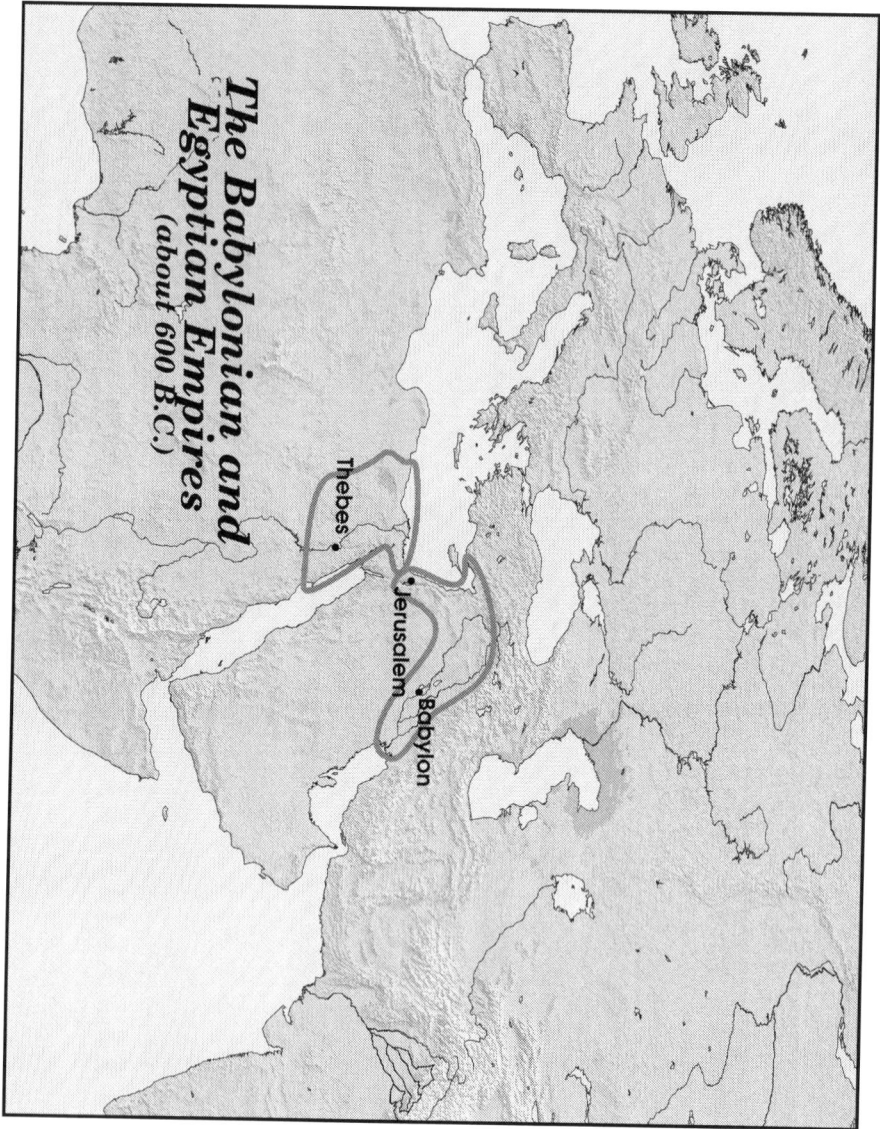

The Babylonian and
Egyptian Empires
(about 600 B.C.)

Thebes

Jerusalem

Babylon

Because of unfaithfulness, God sent the nation of Israel into exile to Babylon. While at Babylon, Daniel saw a series of visions of what was going to happen in world history. From the world's perspective it looked like the Babylonian Empire was impregnable. But Daniel saw that it would shortly be overturned by another.

The Persians swallowed up the Babylonian Empire. It was during this period that, in fulfillment of prophecy, the Persians allowed a faithful remnant to go back to Jerusalem and rebuild the Temple.

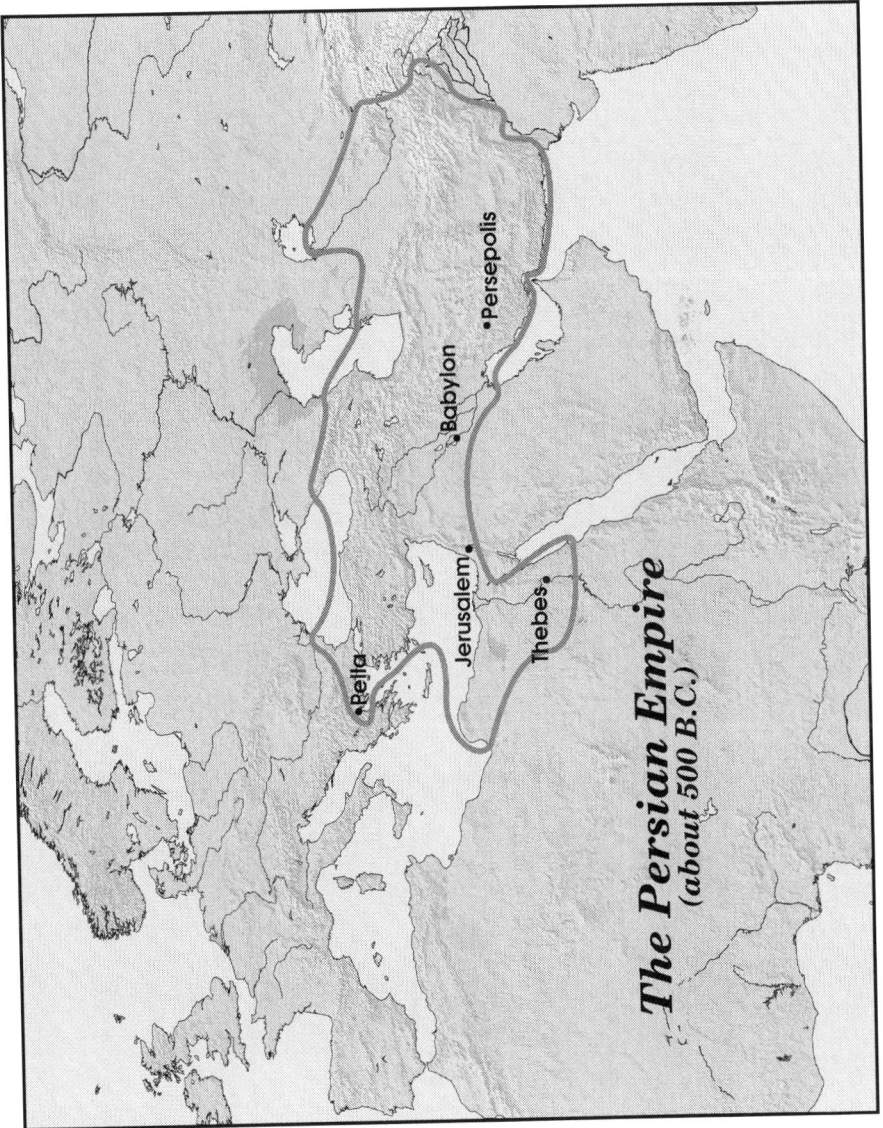

The Persian Empire (about 500 B.C.)

The Persian Empire fell, in turn, to Alexander the Great. In thirteen short years he conquered all the territory up to the borders of India. Then, as foreseen by Daniel, he suddenly died at the height of his power.

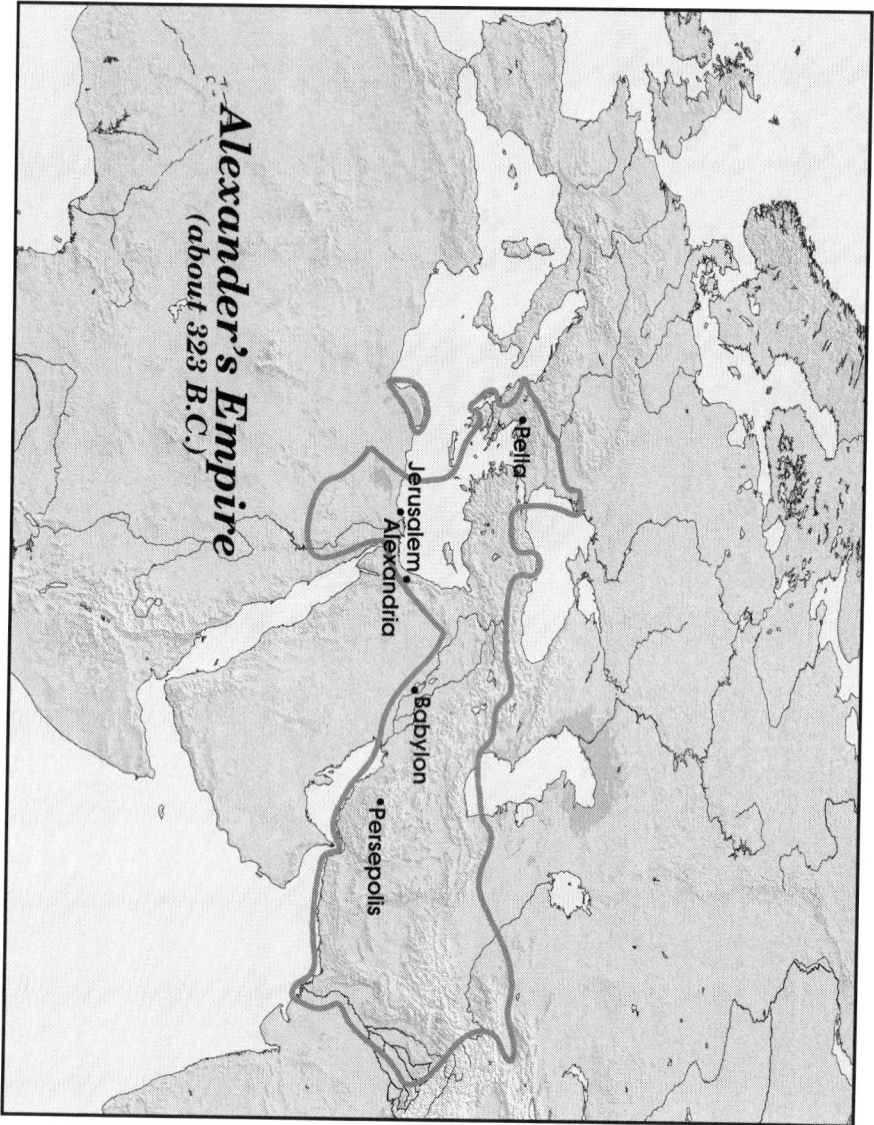

Alexander's Empire (about 323 B.C.)

It is significant that Alexander honored the Jews. Josephus writes that when Alexander marched toward Jerusalem, the High Priest came out to greet him as a fulfillment of prophecy. Alexander was so impressed that he granted the Jews freedom to practice their customs and worship (Antiquities, Book XI, Chapter VIII, 4-5).

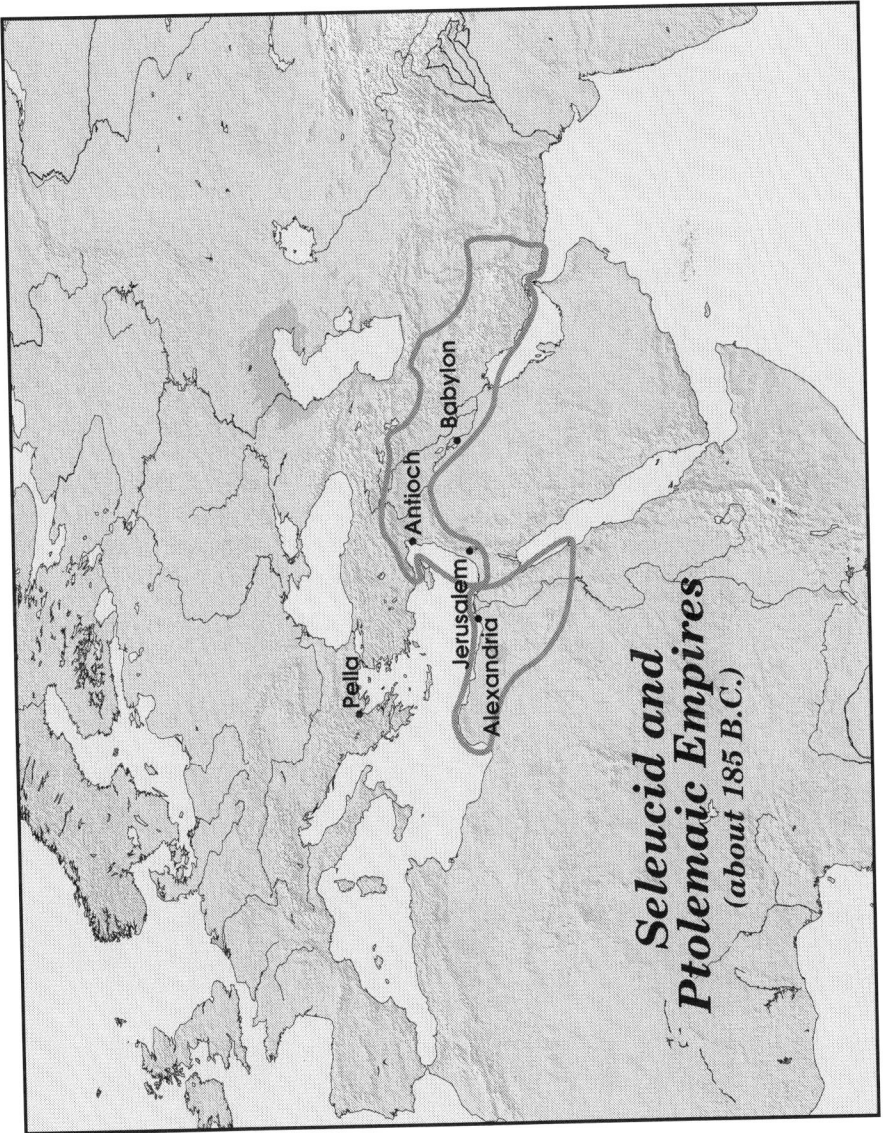

Seleucid and Ptolemaic Empires
(about 185 B.C.)

Alexander's generals broke up his empire into competing sections. From the standpoint of salvation history, the two most important kingdoms to emerge from the breakup were headed by Seleucus and Ptolemy. These two kingdoms struggled for control of Palestine. At first, the Ptolemies gained control. Under their rule the Jewish people enjoyed relative peace and prosperity.

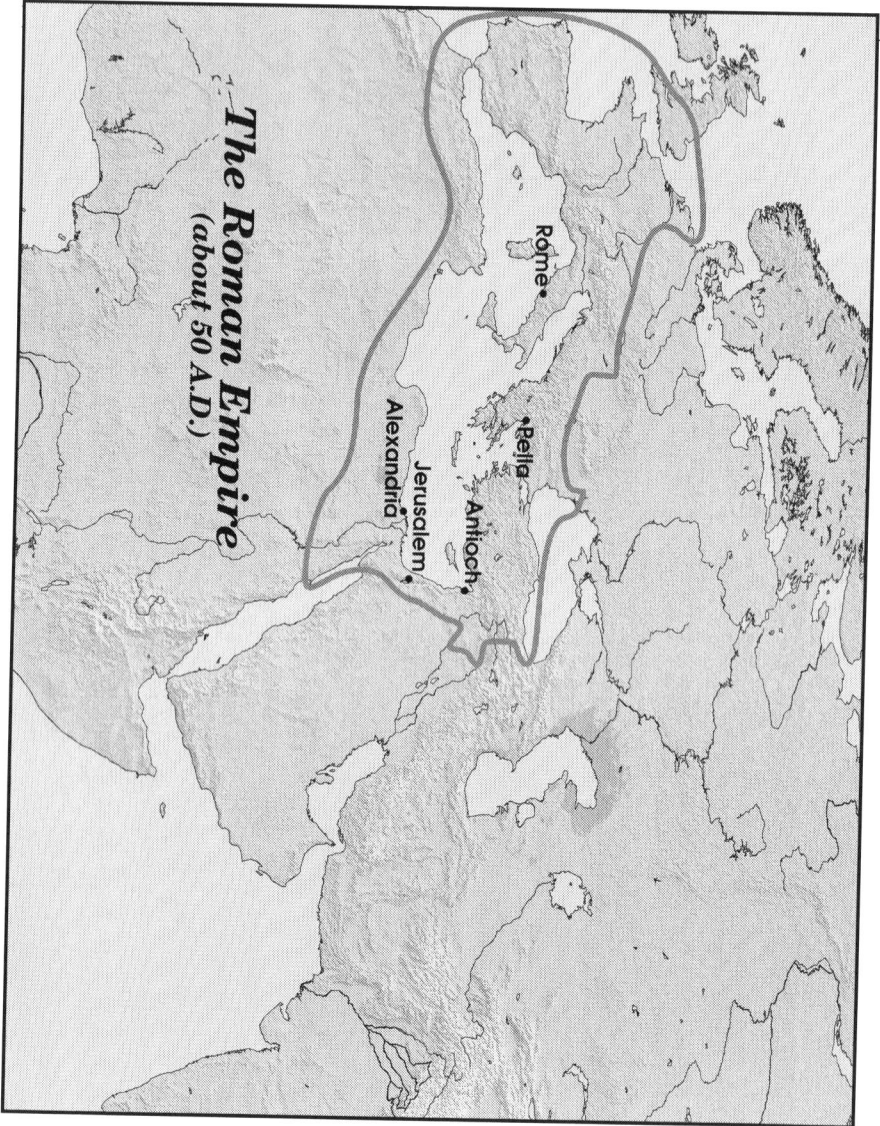

The Roman Empire
(about 50 A.D.)

Rome

Pella

Antioch

Alexandria

Jerusalem

In 166 BC the Jews revolted and after defeating the Syrians in battle after battle, were able to win their independence. Ironically, the Jewish leaders fell to squabbling among themselves. Finally, in 63 BC the Romans intervened. Pompey captured Jerusalem and Jewish rule came to an end. For about the next 100 years, the Romans ruled Palestine through proxy kings. Herod the Great, who was the ruler at the time of Christ's birth, was one of these.

For those who were familiar with the prophecies, it must have been reassuring to see them fulfilled one after another and realize that the time for the coming of the Savior was drawing close. However, Daniel not only saw the succession of world empires, God also gave him a time-table. In Daniel chapter 9, verses 25 through 27 there is a precise indication of when Christ would come. For those who understood the prophecy of the 70 weeks, it must have been exciting to realize that the time had come.

IV.   World Conditions

What sort of world was it into which the Savior was born?

> 1) Because of their exile to Babylon and subsequent events, there were communities of Jewish people scattered throughout the known world. Their presence prepared the way for the Gospel message by bringing people into contact with key concepts and ideas from the Old Testament.

> 2) Alexander had a deliberate policy of spreading Greek culture. One of the significant results of this is that Greek became the universal language of trade and commerce. This common language greatly helped the spread of the Gospel.

Daniel's 70 Weeks
(Daniel 9:25-27)

Ezra returns to Jerusalem - 457 BC

7-7s (49 years)

Rebuilding of Jerusalem complete - 408 BC

62-7s (434 years)

Coming of the Anointed One - 27 AD

Middle of 70th 7

Anointed One "cut off" - 30 AD

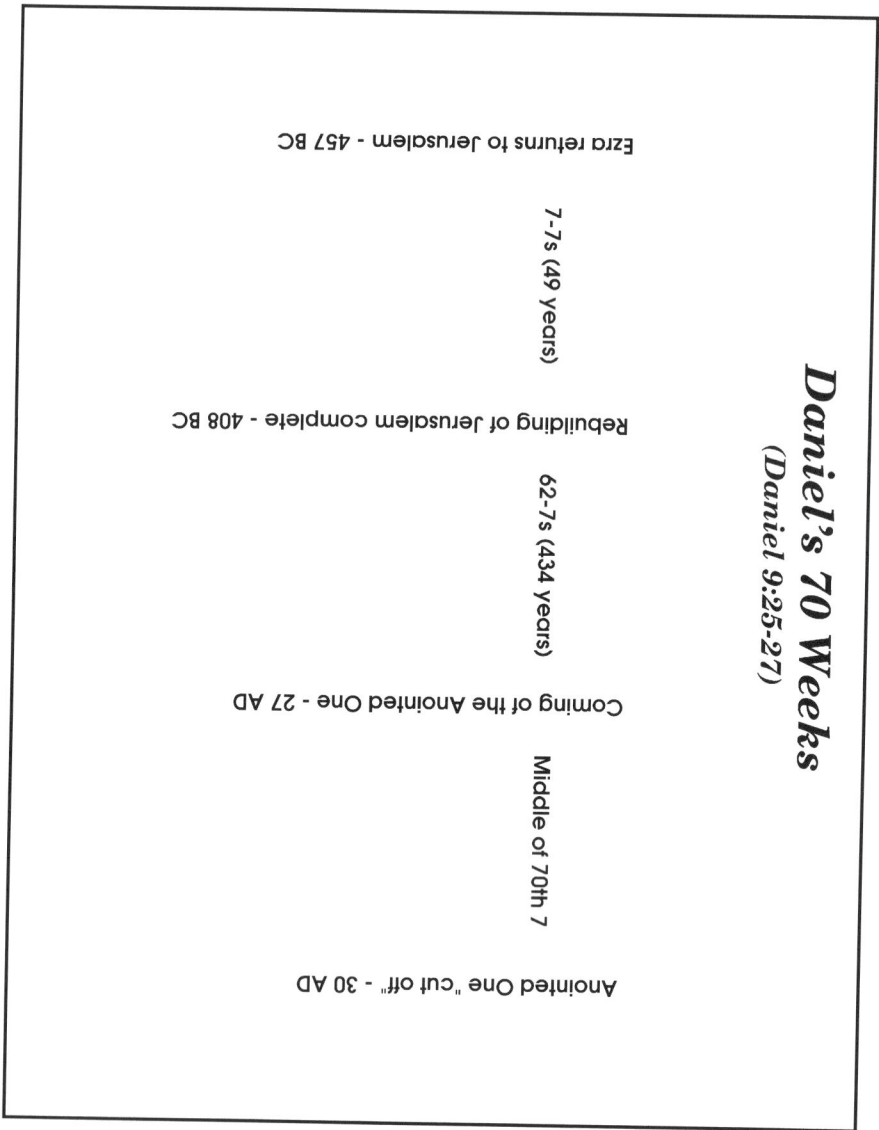

3) The Ptolemies placed a high value on learning. The library at Alexandria was the finest in the world and a center of genuine scholarship. One of the most important events in relation to salvation history was the translation, sponsored by the library, of the Old Testament Scriptures into Greek in the 3rd century BC. This translation (called the Septuagint)

played a crucial role in the spread of the Gospel. Synagogues throughout the Mediterranean region used it. Gentiles who could not read or understand Hebrew now had access to God's word. Just as important, the translation had an effect on the Greek language. The meanings or connotations of many Greek words changed as a result of using them to express Hebrew ideas. In this way Greek speaking people learned new spiritual concepts.

4) The Romans invested a great deal of time and treasure on infrastructure. They are famous for the roads they built – some of which are still in use. Travel became easier than at any previous time in history. This greatly aided the spread of the Gospel.

5) The Roman period was a time of relative stability. Though there was a great deal of turmoil on the borders, there was relative calm within the empire. Political stability and consistent application of laws throughout the empire aided the preaching of the Gospel. For example, more than once, Paul was able to use his status as a Roman citizen to advantage.

6) It was a time when people were heavily influenced by superstitions. The use of spells and incantations was widespread. Magic was big business. For example, see the account in Acts 19:18-19 about burning expensive scrolls used in sorcery. Belief in demonic activity was universal. People believed that sickness and all sorts of calamities were caused by demons. Even highly educated and accomplished people like the Roman general Germanicus were so fearful of the occult powers that they actually willed themselves to death when they thought they had been placed under a curse.

7) It was a time of moral degeneracy. Temple prostitution, both male and female, was universal and accepted. The pleasure gardens of Antioch were world-famous. The promiscuity of the Greek and Roman upper classes is legendary. Plays put on in the theater were lewd and explicit.

8) It was a time of breakdown in the family. Divorce and remarriage was rampant. Incest was common.

9) Little value was placed on human life. Untold thousands died in gladiatorial contests and other blood-sports in the arena. If a newborn didn't meet a father's approval, it would be thrown out along the road to die. Abortion was common.

10) Slavery was widespread. Up to one third of the people in the Roman Empire were slaves.

V.   Parallels

It's interesting to compare our time with those at the birth of Christ. There are a number of similarities.

1) Christian ideas and thought have had a major influence all over the world. Many times people do not even realize that a particular idea or principle is from the Bible, yet it has changed their behavior or belief structure.

2) English has become the universal language of business, commerce and diplomacy. This makes cross-cultural evangelism easier than ever before.

3) Translations of the Scriptures are available in almost every major language.

4) Travel is easier than at any time in history. Air travel has brought most places on the globe only a few hours or days away. Even more importantly, communication is far easier and more universal than ever. The Internet has created new forms of communication and new opportunities.

5) Though our world is torn by strife and conflict, it has been relatively stable ever since World War II. Within broad limits, Americans can travel virtually anywhere they want and enjoy the protection of international law. When they do get into trouble, American embassies around the world can usually help resolve the problem.

6) Belief in magic, the reading of horoscopes, consulting psychics, etc. are all on the rise.

7) Moral degeneracy is on the rise. Promiscuity is rampant. Pornography, x-rated movies and lewd theater shows are everywhere. Homosexuality and prostitution are accepted as normal behaviors.

8) It seems like stable families are the exception. Divorce and remarriage are common. Sexual abuse of children by parents and siblings is everywhere.

9) Little value is placed on human life. Abortion is common-place. Society regards it as a right. People commit murders over trivial things. Violent movies and TV shows are the rule rather than the exception. Blood sports are popular. Shoot-em-up computer games are best-sellers.

10) Slavery is on the rise – particularly in the sex trade.

VI.   A Series Of Visions

A series of visions to various people heralded the coming of the Savior.

> 1) To Zechariah (Luke 1:11-20). An angel foretold the birth of John the baptist, who was to be the forerunner of the Christ.
>
> 2) To Mary (Luke 1:26-38).
>
> 3) To Joseph (Matthew 1:18-21).
>
> 4) To the shepherds (Luke 2:8-15).
>
> 5) To Simeon (Luke 2:25-32).
>
> 6) To the Magi (Matthew 2:1-12).

VII.   Are You Watching?

1) Are we ready for a divine encounter?

What impresses me about all these people is that they were open to hearing God's message even while they were going about the ordinary activities of life. Yes, Zechariah happened to be in the Temple when his encounter occurred. But even he was going about his normal duties and activities. Are we ready for a divine encounter as we go about the tasks of daily living?

What impresses me even more about these people is that they were willing and ready to act on the vision they received. For some of them, it meant accepting considerable risk and inconvenience. Yet all of them obeyed. Zechariah may have been skeptical at first, but when he was convinced that what he experienced was genuine, he accepted it and acted on it. How willing are we to act on the truth we are given? Are we willing to put ourselves at risk to obey the message?

2) Are we looking for the coming of the King?

Just as God gave the Jewish people the promise that a Savior would come one day, He's given us the promise that one day the Savior is coming back. Are we looking for His return? No, we haven't been given a time-table like the one found in Daniel. In fact, Jesus said that nobody knows when the return will be. But would we be surprised if Jesus should come one of these days? Are we eagerly anticipating His return? Are we looking for the fulfillment of the prophecies of the things which must happen before the return?

ഇരുൽ

Obscure Beginnings

Introduction: Galatians 4:4 says, "…when the time had fully come, God sent his Son…" (NIV) Or, as other translations say, "…when the fullness of time had come, God sent forth his Son…" (ESV) The coming of Jesus was not some random event. He came at precisely the right time in history. In the previous study we looked at some of the things which made this the right time.

1) There were Jewish communities throughout the known world. They exposed other cultures and traditions to key concepts and ideas which prepared them to understand the Gospel message.

2) The Greek language had become the universal language of commerce and trade. For the first time since Babel, the peoples of the world could talk to one another easily.

3) The Old Testament Scriptures had been translated into Greek and were widely distributed throughout the entire Mediterranean region.

4) Because of the Roman roads, travel was relatively easy and quick.

5) Due to the Pax Romana, it was a time of relative peace and stability.

6) People were looking for a way out of their moral and spiritual darkness.

I.   Fulfilling Prophecy

Not only did the Savior have to come at the right time, His coming also had to fulfill the prophecies which had been made in the Old Testament Scriptures about His coming. Here are just five of the prophecies Jesus had to fulfill in order to meet the criteria. Some critics claim that Jesus engineered His ministry so that it appeared to fulfill the Old Testament prophecies. It's worth noting that it is impossible for Jesus to have engineered these five.

1) Jesus had to be born of a virgin (Isaiah 7:14). When the angel told Mary she would have a child, she specifically said that she was a virgin (Luke 1:34).

2) He not only had to be physically descended from King David, He had to have a legal claim to the throne. Through Mary, Jesus was a physical descendant of David. In Joseph and Mary the two branches of the kingly line came together. So, no matter how you reckon it, Jesus was the legal heir to the throne.

3) He had to be born in Bethlehem, Judah (Micah 5:2). The census which required everyone to return to their ancestral home took Mary and Joseph to Bethlehem just in time for Jesus' birth (Luke 2:1-7).

4) He had to come from Egypt (Hosea 11:1). Herod's intention to kill Jesus sent Joseph and Mary to Egypt. They returned to Palestine only after a specific instruction from God to do so (Matthew 2:13-21). Incidentally, the gifts the Magi brought (Matthew 2:11) made it possible for the family to flee to Egypt and live there.

5) He had to live in Nazareth, Galilee (Isaiah 11:1). Because Herod's son obtained the throne in Judea, Joseph and Mary went to Galilee on their return from Egypt. They settled in Nazareth (Matthew 2:22-23).

The thing which, perhaps, impresses me most about all this is how it was all balanced on a knife's edge. If even one thing had gone wrong; if only one event had turned out differently, it would have impacted the plan of God beyond calculation.

Another thing which impresses me is how God uses the evil intentions and sins of man to further His plan. For example, Herod tried to destroy the Savior, yet it was his murderous intent which brought about the fulfillment of prophecy.

Question: Do we have the faith to see how God will use the evil we encounter and the sins others commit against us to bring about blessing?

II.   In The Image Of God – Growing In Wisdom

There was a flurry of divine activity around the time of Jesus' birth. As we saw in the previous chapter, at least six different people or groups of people received divine revelations about the birth. However, after the birth, silence descends again. We know almost nothing of Jesus' childhood and early adult years. The Gospels mention only one incident: Jesus' attending Passover in Jerusalem when He was twelve years old (Luke 2:41-52). This incident gives us an interesting insight into Jesus' awareness of who He was and His mission.

Jesus stayed behind in Jerusalem when His parents left to return to Galilee. We don't know why He stayed behind. The account is unclear as to whether Jesus accompanied His parents before on their annual pilgrimages to Jerusalem. If He had, we do not know why this trip was any different in Jesus' mind than any of the others. On the other hand, if this was Jesus' first trip to Jerusalem for Passover, knowing who His heavenly Father was and having some idea of His mission on earth, Jesus may have assumed that His parents were going to leave Him at the Temple as the prophet Samuel's mother had left him at the Tabernacle (1 Samuel 1:20-28).

Incidentally, we learn something about Joseph's and Mary's parenting style from this occurrence. Though they obviously were devout, and cared deeply about their children, they were not the smothering or micro-managing kind of parents. They didn't realize Jesus was missing for a full day. This shows that they trusted their son to do the right thing and didn't worry about what mischief He might be up to. It also tells us something about Jesus. He was a trustworthy child. He generally didn't give his parents anything to worry about.

We don't know at what age Jesus began to understand who He was. It's clear that by age twelve He knew that God was His heavenly Father. "...Didn't you know I had to be in my Father's house?" (Luke 2:49 NIV) It seems that He also had some idea that He was to have a special role in God's plan, but He obviously did not fully understand the role or the timing. Another eighteen years had to pass before the time was right for Him to begin His ministry. In the meantime, He had to return to Nazareth and obey His parents. This lesson was to stand Him in good stead later in life. Hebrews 5:8 says, "Although he was a son, he learned obedience from what he suffered" (NIV). No doubt the lesson in obedience Jesus learned at age twelve helped Him face the much harder tests of obedience later on.

The fact that Jesus had to learn brings up an intriguing question. Luke 2:52 says that Jesus "...grew [or increased] in wisdom..." (NIV) This means that He did not have as much wisdom as a boy as He did as a young adult or as a man. Yet, since Jesus is Immanuel, "God with us" (Matthew 1:23) how can this be? If Jesus is divine – and Scripture is plain that He is – why would He need to grow in wisdom? Being God, wouldn't Jesus already possess all wisdom, along with the other attributes of God?

Colossians 2:9 provides the answer to this dilemma, "For in Christ all the fullness of the Deity lives in bodily form," (NIV). The key is the phrase 'bodily form.' Yes, Jesus is God in the flesh, but in order for Him to take on a physical body, He had to leave certain aspects or dimensions of divinity behind. He had to accept the limitations inherent in the medium. Only so much of God can fit in the package of a human body. Philippians 2:5-7 explains it this way, "Your attitude should be the same as that of Christ Jesus: Who, being in very nature God, did not consider equality with God something to be grasped, but made himself nothing, taking the very nature of a servant, being made in human likeness." (NIV)

According to this verse, in comparison to the nature of God, the nature of a human being is nothing. Not very much of God can fit or be expressed in the form of a human body. Also, the capacity of the human form is much different at various stages of life. So, while Jesus was a baby, He displayed as much of the fullness of God as a baby is capable of containing. As His physical body grew and developed, its capacity to contain more of the fullness of God also increased. The boy was more capable than the baby and the man more capable than the boy.

Hebrews 1:3 expresses the concept with a different metaphor. "The Son is the radiance of God's glory and the exact representation [or image] of his being…" (NIV) The idea of representation or image can help us understand why Jesus had limitations even though He is God in the flesh. Suppose you take a digital picture of your car. The image may be absolutely perfect, yet it is very different than the reality it represents. For example, the car is material – it is composed of physical matter. In contrast, the image has no material existence – it is composed of 1s and 0s which are, themselves, merely expressions of an idea. The car has some sort of motor, the image does not. And so forth. In the same way, though Jesus is the perfect image of God, the medium is very limited.

Did Jesus have to learn right from wrong? Did He ever make mistakes as a child? Scripture does not answer questions like this directly. However, there are two things we do know for certain: 1) Jesus never sinned. 2) Jesus was tempted in every way that we are (Hebrews 4:15). This means that as a baby Jesus overcame whatever temptations babies face. As a boy He overcame whatever temptations boys face. The same holds true for when He was a young adult and a man. He faced it all, and always did the right thing. He did not sin.

This doesn't mean that Jesus already knew everything and how to act. No doubt He had to learn the social graces, just like everybody else. No doubt He had to learn to work and use tools just like every other human. No doubt He had to go to school and learn how to read, just like other boys. Since Scripture says He was tempted in all ways, I wouldn't be surprised if, in some area, Jesus had a learning disability. There was probably something which did not come easily to Him.

III.   Fulfilling Righteousness

After the incident in Jerusalem, silence again descends on Jesus' life for another eighteen years. We catch our next glimpse of Him when He was about thirty (Luke 3:23).

John the Baptist, who was Jesus' cousin, came preaching a message of repentance. He also baptized those who did repent. I want to stress that immersion was nothing new. For centuries the Jews had been immersing themselves as part of their ritual cleansing ceremonies.

What was new in this case was that it was John who did the baptizing, instead of a person immersing himself (Matthew 3:6, Mark 1:5).

The other thing which was new is that John linked baptism with the concept of death. The Greek word which the New Testament uses for baptism a form of the word 'baptizo' (βαπτιζω). The Greeks never used this word for a ritual or ceremonial cleansing. This particular form of the word had a bad connotation. Though it still meant 'to immerse,' people associated it with disaster or destruction. They used it to describe things like drowning or a ship going under. Never before had ritual cleansing in water been linked with the concept of death.

In this context it's no wonder that John was startled when Jesus came to be baptized. John apparently had enough spiritual awareness to know that Jesus had nothing to repent of. He was sinless. Since He was sinless, why was he asking to be baptized? John felt that it should be the other way around. It would be more appropriate for Jesus to baptize him (Matthew 3:14).

Jesus replied that it was necessary for John to baptize Him "to fulfill all righteousness" (Matthew 3:15). What does this mean?

> When we think of righteousness, we contrast it with unrighteousness. In other words, we think of it as the opposite of sin. But in Scripture the concept of righteousness is much broader than that. One of the attributes of God is that He is righteous (Ezra 9:15, Psalm 116:5, Isaiah 45:21, etc.). Not only is God, Himself, righteous, His laws, commands and word are righteous (Psalm 119). With this in mind, we can define 'righteousness' as fulfilling the purpose or will of God. Jesus asked to be baptized, not because He was a sinner in need of forgiveness for sins, but in order to fulfill God's will.

What role or function did Jesus' baptism have in fulfilling God's purpose? There were probably many purposes but I think the two main ones are as follows:

1) One purpose for Jesus' baptism has to do with the idea of repentance. Remember that John's baptism was a baptism of repentance. We can think of repentance as dying to our previous lifestyle. No, Jesus had no sins or bad habits to repent of but, from this point on, His life was going to be radically different than it was before. He was turning his back on the building trade and the carpenter shop in Nazareth. From this point on, His entire attention was going to be focused on fulfilling the mission God sent Him to accomplish. In His baptism, He was dying to His old life.

2) Even more importantly, it was at His baptism that Jesus received His divine commission. As soon as Jesus was baptized, the Spirit came upon Him. In addition to the Spirit, a voice came from heaven, "…This is my Son, whom I love; with him I am well pleased." (Matthew 3:17 NIV) What is the significance? I think it is safe to say that Jesus received His anointing at His baptism. Jesus implied as much when He read from Isaiah at the synagogue at Nazareth. "The scroll of the prophet Isaiah was handed to him. Unrolling it, he found the place where it is written: "The Spirit of the Lord is on me, because he has anointed me to preach good news to the poor. He has sent me to proclaim freedom for the prisoners and recovery of sight for the blind, to release the oppressed, to proclaim the year of the Lord's favor." Then he rolled up the scroll, gave it back to the attendant and sat down. The eyes of everyone in the synagogue were fastened on him, and he began by saying to them, "Today this scripture is fulfilled in your hearing."" (Luke 4:17-21 NIV)

Peter indicated the same thing at the house of Cornelius, "You know what has happened throughout Judea, beginning in Galilee after the baptism that John preached – how God anointed Jesus of Nazareth with the Holy Spirit and power, and how he went around doing good and healing all who were under the power of the devil, because God was with him." (Acts 10:37-38 NIV)

The Spirit came on Jesus at His baptism. It was then that God commissioned Him to do His ministry and it was then that He received the power to do it.

But wasn't Jesus born 'king of the Jews' (Matthew 2:1-2)? Wasn't He identified as the Savior, Christ and Lord at His birth (Luke 2:11)? If so, how can we say that He received His anointing at His baptism? Perhaps an analogy with a physical kingdom will help clarify the situation. Suppose an heir is born to an earthly king. Though he is royalty; though he will inherit the kingdom; though he is born to be king, he does not become the king until he goes through the investiture ceremony. In the same way, though He was born to be the Christ, Jesus did not actually become the Christ until His anointing at His baptism.

IV.   Second Adam

Right after His anointing, Jesus went through a period of testing. Mark records that, after His baptism, the Spirit immediately sent Jesus into the desert (Mark 1:12). Matthew says that the purpose was to be tempted by the devil (Matthew 4:1). Why?

The key is probably contained in the Scriptures Jesus quoted while refuting the devil. The temptations Jesus endured parallel the experiences the Israelites went through in the wilderness. The forty days of temptation correspond to the forty years of wandering. God called Israel, His son (for example see Exodus 4:22-23). Where the type, or forerunner, failed, the true Son overcame. Jesus, therefore, is the fulfillment of God's purpose and expectation for the nation of Israel.

The first temptation had to do with physical needs. According to Deuteronomy 8, God tested the Israelites with hunger so they would learn to depend upon God. "Remember how the LORD your God led you all the way in the desert these forty years, to humble you and to test you in order to know what was in your heart, whether or not you would keep his commands. He humbled you, causing you to hunger and then feeding you with manna, which neither you nor your fathers had known, to teach you that man does not live on bread alone but on every word that comes from the mouth of the LORD." (Deuteronomy 8:2-3 NIV) The Israelites failed the test time after time. Jesus, the true Son of God, passed it. He would rely on God's word and be obedient regardless of whether he had physical food or not.

The next test had to do with faith. Is God really with you or not? The Israelites questioned whether God was with them. Exodus 17:1-7 says, "The whole Israelite community set out from the Desert of Sin, traveling from place to place as the LORD commanded. They camped at Rephidim, but there was no water for the people to drink. So they quarreled with Moses and said, "Give us water to drink." Moses replied, "Why do you quarrel with me? Why do you put the LORD to the test?" But the people were thirsty for water there, and they grumbled against Moses. They said, "Why did you bring us up out of Egypt to make us and our children and livestock die of thirst?" Then Moses cried out to the LORD, "What am I to do with these people? They are almost ready to stone me." The LORD answered Moses, "Walk on ahead of the people. Take with you some of the elders of Israel and take in your hand the staff with which you struck the Nile, and go. I will stand there before you by the rock at Horeb. Strike the rock, and water will come out of it for the people to drink." So Moses did this in the sight of the elders of Israel. And he called the place Massah and Meribah because the Israelites quarreled and because they tested the LORD saying, "Is the LORD among us or not?"" (NIV)

Jesus refused to test God. In refuting the devil He quoted from Deuteronomy 6:16 which says, "Do not test the LORD your God as you did at Massah." (NIV)

The third temptation had to with worship. Though the Israelites had repeatedly been told to worship God alone, and they had promised to so, they often fell into idolatry. Jesus turned the temptation aside by quoting Deuteronomy 6:13: "Fear the LORD your God, serve him only and take your oaths in his name." (NIV)

It's ironic that the devil used the wealth and splendor of the kingdoms of the world as the incentive to try to buy Jesus' worship.

As God's anointed King, it all belongs to Jesus anyway. But He was willing to wait for God's timing. He would not go against God's will in order to gain instant gratification. He would not give up the eternal to gain the immediate. Because He refused to bow to the devil, the day is coming when every knee will bow to Him.

There is another dimension to the temptations, as well. Luke records the genealogy of Jesus just before the temptation account. He ends it with "…the son of Adam, the son of God." (Luke 3:38) It's possible that Luke is contrasting the first Adam, with the second. The first Adam succumbed to temptation. Jesus, the second Adam, did not. Through Jesus, the curse which came on mankind because of Adam would be reversed. Paul writes, "For since death came through a man, the resurrection of the dead comes also through a man. For as in Adam all die, so in Christ all will be made alive." (1 Corinthians 15:21-22 NIV)

V.   Overcoming

In this chapter we've spoken quite a bit about temptation. What was it that enabled Jesus to overcome it? I suggest two things:

1) Jesus had an ever-present awareness of God. Even from an early age He was aware that God was His heavenly Father. The more we are conscious of God's presence and His love for us, the less likely we will be to do things which are against His will.

2) The Scriptures were not an abstraction to Jesus. They were living words which applied to daily life. Jesus was thoroughly aware of what Scripture said and was able to counter the things the devil threw at Him by referring to them. The more we become familiar with the principles of Scripture, the more we will be able to apply them to specific situations which come up in our lives.

೮೦೦೮

Ministry in Obscurity

Introduction: We tend to think of Jesus beginning His ministry suddenly, with no special training or obvious preparation for the role He took on for the next 3-1/2 years. In reality, Jesus spent 30 years preparing for His ministry. As we saw before, one of the crucial things Jesus had to learn during those years was the lesson of obedience. Learning to obey His parents prepared Jesus for the much harder test of obeying His heavenly Father's will when it was time to face the cross.

Though Jesus was born to be King, God did not commission Him until His baptism. It was at His baptism that God anointed Him with the Spirit and with power. After His baptism Jesus could legitimately be called the Christ. But, immediately following His anointing, the Christ faced a vicious challenge from the Devil. Jesus overcame all the temptations the Devil threw at Him by resorting to Scripture. In doing so, Jesus, God's Son, fulfilled God's purpose and expectation for that other son, the nation of Israel. As the 'second Adam' Jesus also reversed the experience of the first Adam.

Jesus must have spent some time recovering from His ordeal. After 40 days of fasting, He would have been in no shape to travel all over Palestine teaching and tending to the needs of other people. However, the only hint the Scriptures give us of this recovery period is that angels ministered to Him (Matthew 4:11, Mark 1:13).

After Jesus recovered from the temptation, He returned to the scene where John had baptized Him. (Presumably this was "Bethany on the other side of the Jordan" (John 1:28).)

I.   John's Ministry

When we look at Jesus' ministry, it's amazing what He was able to accomplish in just 3-1/2 years. Yet, it is probably fair to say that Jesus could not have done it in that short amount of time if it hadn't been for John the Baptist.

What was the purpose of John's ministry?

John's ministry can be summed up in the words, preparation, proclamation and identification.

Preparation: All four of the Gospels associate Isaiah's prophecy from chapter 40:3-5, with John: For example, Luke writes, "As is written in the book of the words of Isaiah the prophet: "A voice of one calling in the desert, 'Prepare the way for the Lord, make straight paths for him. Every valley shall be filled in, every mountain and hill made low. The crooked roads shall become straight, the rough ways smooth. And all mankind will see God's salvation.'" (Luke 3:4-6 NIV)

How did John prepare the way? How did he make the paths straight and smooth for Jesus?

One of the things John did was to prepare people's hearts to receive Jesus' message.

How did he do this? What was John's message?

John's message was, "...Repent, for the kingdom of heaven is near." (Matthew 3:2 NIV) He awoke in people a realization that they were sinners in need of forgiveness. He also taught that true repentance would demonstrate itself in action and a changed lifestyle (Matthew 3:8, Luke 3:8-14). Because of their acting on John's teaching, people could accept Jesus' teaching more readily (Luke 7:29-30).

Proclamation: John not only taught a message of repentance, he consistently said that he was not the Messiah. Though he, himself, was not the Messiah, the Messiah's coming was near (Matthew 3:11-12, Mark 1:7-8, Luke 3:15-17, John 1:26-27). John's proclamation of the Messiah awoke an expectation among the people and made them more ready to accept Jesus when He came. For example John writes, "Then Jesus went back across the Jordan to the place where John had been baptizing in the early days. Here he stayed and many people came to him. They said, "Though John never performed a miraculous sign, all that John said about this man was true." And in that place many believed in Jesus." (John 10:40-42 NIV)

Identification: John not only said that the Savior was coming, he identified Jesus as that Savior. In fact, John said that the purpose of his ministry was to make this identification. "The next day John saw Jesus coming toward him and said, "Look, the Lamb of God, who takes away the sin of the world! This is the one I meant when I said, 'A man who comes after me has surpassed me because he was before me.' I myself did not know him, but the reason I came baptizing with water was that he might be revealed to Israel.'" (John 1:29-31 NIV)

II.   The First Disciples

The immediate effect of John pointing out Jesus as the Savior, was that it gave Jesus a following. Some of John's disciples became disciples of Jesus. This was, no doubt, precisely what John intended. The whole point of his ministry was to direct people to Christ. From John, chapter 1 we know who five of the first disciples were: John, Andrew, Simon Peter, Philip and Nathanael. We know that at least 2, and perhaps all 5, of the first followers of Christ were disciples of John. It's significant that of the 5, 4 of them became Apostles.

In the calling of these first disciples we also see a pattern of discipleship which is still valid today. The progression is: "Come and see" (John 1:39, 46), Experience (John1:39, 45, 47-48), Follow (John 1:43), Invite others (John 1:41, 45). Later on, Jesus would make explicit other conditions of discipleship. Namely, "Count the cost" (Luke 14:27-33), "Deny yourself" (Matthew 16:24, Mark 8:34, Luke 9:23) and "Leave" (Matthew 8:22, Luke 9:60).

III.   Beginning Of The Signs

With His new disciples in tow, Jesus left Judea and traveled to Cana, in Galilee where they were invited to attend a wedding. There Jesus performed the first of what John calls signs, by changing water into wine.

What are the signs? There are 8 miracles or signs listed in the Gospel of John.

1) Changing water into wine (John 2:1-11).

2) Healing the official's son (John 4:43-54).

3) The healing at the pool of Bethesda (John 5:1-15).

4) The feeding of the 5,000 (John 6:1-14).

5) Walking on water (John 6:16-21).

6) Healing of the man born blind (John 9:1-12).

7) The raising of Lazarus from the dead (John 11:1-44).

8) The miraculous catch of fish (John 21:1-14).

What was the intent or purpose of the signs? What were they intended to show?

Each one of the signs revealed some aspect of Jesus' identity or position. The intent was to confront the witnesses with the decision to accept or reject God's Messiah.

1) Jesus revealed His glory (John 2:11).

2) Jesus is Lord over time, distance and disease (John 4:53).

3) Jesus is Lord of the Sabbath, and the Son of God (John 5:16-18).

4) Jesus is the bread of life (John 6:35).

5) Jesus is sovereign over nature (John 6:19-21).

6) Jesus is the light of the world (John 9:5).

7) Jesus is the resurrection and the life (John 11:25).

8) Jesus is the resurrected Lord (John 21:12).

Each one of these incidents called for a response of faith. Some believed and took action on the basis of the sign, others refused to believe in spite of the evidence.

After changing the water into wine at Cana, Jesus and His disciples spent a brief time in Capernaum. Then, at the Passover season, they left for Jerusalem.

IV.   1st Passover

During the 1st Passover of Jesus' ministry two important events occurred. The first of these events was cleansing the Temple. The religious authorities had desecrated the Temple by turning it into a place of business.

What was God's intended purpose for the Temple?

1) The Temple was a visual expression of God's covenant relationship with the people of Israel. Tradition says that the Ark of the Covenant (the box in which a copy of the Covenant – the Ten Commandments – was kept) was no longer in the Holy of Holies of the Temple which existed at the time of Jesus' ministry. It supposedly had been hidden somewhere in the Temple Mount at the time of the Babylonian Captivity. Nevertheless, the Covenant and the Mercy Seat – the lid on top of the Ark on which the blood of the annual sin sacrifice was sprinkled – were the focal point of the entire Jewish religion.

2) The Temple was to serve as an invitation to non-Jewish peoples to enter into the Covenant with God. In Isaiah 56:7 the Temple is called "a house of prayer for all nations." (NIV) In other words, it was to be a place where all people could come and pray. This was the purpose for the Court of the Gentiles. Even those who had not yet become part of the Covenant people could worship according to the knowledge they had.

By making the Temple a place of business, the authorities, a) diverted people's attention away from their relationship to God and, b) made it difficult or impossible for Gentiles to come near to

Him. By clearing out the Temple, Jesus forced everyone to re-assess their priorities.

Jesus' cleansing the Temple should have been a clear indication of who He was to those who were Scripturally aware. Malachi 3:1-4 says, ""See, I will send my messenger, who will prepare the way before me. Then suddenly the Lord you are seeking will come to his temple; the messenger of the covenant, whom you desire, will come," says the LORD Almighty. But who can endure the day of his coming? Who can stand when he appears? For he will be like a refiner's fire or a launderer's soap. He will sit as a refiner and purifier of silver; he will purify the Levites and refine them like gold and silver. Then the LORD will have men who will bring offerings in righteousness, and the offerings of Judah and Jerusalem will be acceptable to the LORD, as in days gone by, as in former years." (NIV)

Jesus' reply to those who questioned His authority to cleanse the Temple also points to Himself as the ultimate fulfillment of the Temple. Remember that this incident took place during the Passover. Jesus was going to offer Himself as the perfect sacrifice to take away sins, for all time. The animal sacrifices were going to come to an end. All would look to Jesus, rather than the Temple as the focus of their covenant relationship with God.

The second incident the Gospels record during this visit to Jerusalem is Jesus' conversation with Nicodemus. During this conversation Nicodemus mentions the miracles that Jesus had been performing. Jesus must have done several during His time in Jerusalem, but we do not have a record of them (see John 4:45).

In this conversation, Jesus stressed the need for a new birth – not a physical one, but one of water and the Spirit. Also, for the first time Jesus expressed the purpose of His coming – to save the world (John 3:17). Salvation, however, is conditional. Only those who believe will attain it. Those who refuse to believe will be condemned.

We don't know how long Jesus spent in Jerusalem. Sometime after the Passover, He took His disciples into the countryside (John 3:22).

We don't know much about this time except that He apparently taught His disciples to baptize (compare John 3:22 with John 4:1-2).

During this period, John's disciples got upset because Jesus was gaining more disciples than John. Unfortunately, they had missed the whole point of John's ministry. It was to clear the way for, and point people to, Jesus. In his reply, John demonstrated the classic attitude of a spiritual leader, "He must become greater, I must become less." (John 3:30 NIV)

V.   Return To Galilee

When Jesus learned that the Pharisees had heard that He was gaining disciples, He left Judea and returned to Galilee. On the way He went through Samaria. At Jacob's well, He had another one of those conversations which so brilliantly illuminate what true spirituality is. True worship is not confined to a particular place, but to a particular type of person. It is those who worship in spirit and truth whom God is looking for (John 4:23-24). Also, in this conversation Jesus, for the first time, declared Himself as the Christ (John 4:25-26). This was particularly remarkable because He made the declaration not only to a woman, which in Jewish thought was bad enough, but to an immoral woman, and one of a despised race (John 4:9, 17-18, 27). Jesus was clearly indicating that the message of forgiveness and acceptance was for all people.

The woman at the well is another example of the pattern of discipleship we see in the calling of the first 5 disciples. After her experience with Jesus, she invited others to come and see (John 4:29). They, in turn, experienced Him, and believed (John 4:39-42).

Upon His return to Galilee, Jesus encountered an official from Capernaum whose son was deathly ill. Jesus healed the son at a distance. John writes that this was the second sign that Jesus performed (John 4:54). One of the interesting things about it is that it seems, to a certain degree, to have been contingent on the man's believing what Jesus told him. "…The man took Jesus at his word and departed." (John 4:50 NIV). That belief led to a further and deeper belief when the man learned that his son was cured. Once again we see the pattern of discipleship. Experience with Jesus leads a person to invite others to share that experience (John 4:53).

VI.   Choosing A Base Of Operations

Though the Galileans welcomed Jesus (Luke 4:14-15, John 4:45), the welcome was not universal. Jesus went to Nazareth, the place where He had grown up. There, in the synagogue, Jesus declared who He was by referring to a prophecy of Isaiah. At first the message was well received (Luke 4:22). But when Jesus started to apply it, the people became so angry that they tried to kill him (Luke 4:29-30).

Because of rejection in His home town, Jesus had to move His base of operations. He chose Capernaum (Matthew 4:12-16, Luke 4:31). We aren't told the reasons why Jesus happened to pick this particular town on the Sea of Galilee. Possibly it was because several people who already believed in Him lived there. There was the official whose son Jesus had healed, and his household. Though Peter, Andrew and Philip originally came from Bethsaida (John 1:44), the Gospels seem to imply that Peter and Andrew lived in Capernaum (Mark 1:29-30, Luke 4:38). If this is true, then Capernaum was a logical place for Jesus to go after being thrown out of Nazareth. In any case, Capernaum seems to be the place Jesus called 'home' during the rest of His ministry.

V.   Choices

Jesus is far more than a great teacher. His words and actions continually confront us with a choice: Will we believe that He is the Messiah, the Son of God, or will we refuse to believe? Will we act on our belief? Will we become a disciple, or will we refuse to follow? As a disciple will we invite others to come and experience Jesus?

ഇൻ

Proclaiming the Kingdom

Introduction: After being rejected in Nazareth, Jesus selected the town of Capernaum on the Sea of Galilee as His base of operations. Commentators sometimes call the year following Jesus' move to Capernaum the "Great Galilean Ministry." It was during this year that Jesus emerged from obscurity. News about Him spread, not only throughout Palestine but, even to the surrounding regions.

What were the characteristics of this period?

1) Except for one visit to Jerusalem, Jesus spent most of His time in Galilee.

2) During the first part of this period, Jesus toured from town to town in Galilee preaching in the synagogues. However, the accounts emphasize the miracles and healings which Jesus performed.

3) It was a time when Jesus enjoyed immense popularity. Crowds numbering in the thousands followed Him about. The demands on Jesus were so heavy that, at times, He and His disciples did not even have the opportunity to eat (Mark 3:20, 6:31).

4) Though Jesus was immensely popular, opposition to His teaching also began to appear, particularly in Jerusalem.

5) It was a time of training. It was during this period that Jesus selected and taught the men who would carry on His ministry.

6) It was a time of public teaching. Later on in His ministry, Jesus would concentrate on teaching His close disciples. But at this stage, Jesus spent a lot of time teaching and preaching to the crowds. As we shall see, the emphasis of the teaching was on the character and ethics of the Kingdom of God.

I.   The Ministry Of Healing

Of the total number of miracles Jesus performed, the Gospels record only a few. The accounts indicate that the number of people Jesus healed probably numbered in the hundreds, if not thousands.

What was the purpose, or intent, of the miracles?

> One thing we know for sure is that Jesus did not perform miracles or heal people in order to attract crowds or to gain notoriety. We know this because, on several occasions, He told people not to tell others about what He had done (Mark 5:43, 7:36, Luke 5:14, 8:56). This is quite a contrast to the so-called faith healers and miracle workers of today who like to draw attention to themselves.

> If the purpose of the miracles was not to draw attention then what were they for? As we saw in the last chapter, they acted as signs. In other words, they showed something about the nature and identity of Jesus. They were intended to open people's eyes to greater truth or understanding.

> The miracles were also Jesus' authenticator. They were proof that He came from God – that He was working in the power of God. "The Jews gathered around him, saying, "How long will you keep us in suspense? If you are the Christ, tell us plainly." Jesus answered, "I did tell you, but you do not believe. The miracles I do in my Father's name speak for me,"" (John 10:24-25 NIV) Another time He said, "Believe me when I say that I am in the Father and the Father is in me; or at least believe on the evidence of the miracles themselves." (John 14:11 NIV)

> The records we have indicate that Jesus never healed at random. It was either as a result of a specific request, He took pity on someone who was in no condition to ask for help, or Jesus performed a miracle to make a specific spiritual point.

Jesus' miracles of healing began to gain widespread attention as a result of events in Capernaum. One Sabbath He healed a demon-possessed man in the synagogue (Mark 1:21-27, Luke 4:31-36).

Following this, Jesus healed Peter's mother-in-law of a fever (Matthew 8:14-15, Mark 1:29-31, Luke 4:38-39). This triggered an avalanche of sick, seeking to get well (Matthew 8:16-17, Mark 1:32-34, Luke 4:40-41). From this point on, it was difficult for Jesus to go anywhere without being besieged by the sick.

After performing the healings at Capernaum, Jesus made a tour of Galilee (Matthew 4:23-25, Mark 1:35-39, Luke 4:42-44). Sometime during this tour Jesus healed a leper (Matthew 8:1-4, Mark 1:40-45, Luke 5:12-16).

One of the most spectacular cures occurred after Jesus returned to Capernaum. Jesus was teaching in someone's house when some men opened a hole in the roof and lowered a paralytic down in front of him (Matthew 9:2-8, Mark 2:3-12, Luke 5:18-26). Not only was the method of getting this man to Jesus startling, but Jesus' response to the man was startling, as well. He used the opportunity to teach an extremely important lesson about Himself. Before healing the man, He forgave the man's sins. This was a clear demonstration, not only of Jesus' power to perform miracles, but of His divine authority and identity. Only God can forgive.

Sometime after this incident, John tells us that Jesus traveled to Jerusalem for one of the Jewish feasts (John 5:1). He doesn't say which feast this was. It's possible it was Passover. If so, this would have been a year since Jesus had cleansed the Temple. While Jesus was in Jerusalem, He healed a paralytic at the pool of Bethesda (John 5:2-15). Since the healing took place on the Sabbath, this brought Jesus into sharp controversy with the Jewish authorities. During the exchange Jesus identified God as His Father (John 5:16-18). It was these two things: Breaking their customs regarding the Sabbath, and claiming to be God's Son, which the Jewish authorities could not tolerate. It was these two things, plus Jesus' challenge to the Temple – identifying Himself as the true Temple – which caused them to seek His death.

It's interesting that the next two incidents the Gospels record, also involved breaking the Sabbath traditions. They apparently took place after Jesus returned to Galilee. The first involved plucking and eating some grain while Jesus and His disciples were walking on the

Sabbath (Matthew 12:1-8, Mark 2:23-28, Luke 6:1-5). When challenged, Jesus pointed out that there was another principle in the Law which modified the strict interpretation about not doing work on the Sabbath. Then He declared that He was the Lord of the Sabbath.

The other incident was healing a man with a withered hand (Matthew 12:9-14, Mark 3:1-6, Luke 6:6-11). Again, Jesus acted on the intent of the Law, rather than the letter of it.

II.   Selecting Witnesses

In addition to teaching publicly and healing, Jesus also used this time to select certain men for special training. There is some ambiguity as to the order of events and when Jesus called the disciples, because the Gospel accounts list the events in different order. What follows is according to Luke's chronology.

We need to back up a little to when Jesus healed Peter's mother-in-law. That night Jesus healed many of the sick in Capernaum. Then, early in the morning, He went by Himself to a solitary place. When Peter and the others found Him, Jesus declared His intent to leave and preach in the other towns of Galilee. What happened next is not entirely clear. Mark indicates that Jesus invited Peter and the others to go along with Him (Mark 1:35-39). Luke does not mention Peter by name, but records people trying to keep Jesus from leaving (Luke 4:42-44). The implication is that these people stayed at Capernaum, while Jesus left on His tour of Galilee. Putting the two accounts together, it's possible that Jesus invited Peter and the other disciples to come on the tour. They, in turn, urged Jesus to stay at Capernaum. Then, Jesus left while the disciples stayed behind.

In any case, the next glimpse we have of Peter, Andrew, James and John is of them washing their nets in the Sea of Galilee after having fished all night with no catch (Matthew 4:18-22, Mark 1:16-20, Luke 5:1-11). Jesus borrowed Peter's boat and used it as a platform from which to teach the crowd. After teaching the people, Jesus asked Peter to cast the nets. Peter reluctantly did so and the resulting catch was so big that it threatened to sink his boat as well as the boat of his partners.

Apparently, it was this incident which convinced Peter of who Jesus really was. At least he recognized his own sinfulness in comparison to Jesus. This time, when Jesus asked Peter and the others to come, they didn't hesitate. They beached their boats and followed. From then on, they stayed with Jesus until the end.

The fishermen weren't the only ones Jesus invited to follow Him. We know of at least two others. One man pleaded family obligations as an excuse for not following (Luke 9:59). The other person was a wealthy young man who was too attached to his money (Matthew 19:21-22, Mark 10:21-22, Luke 18:22-23). Others volunteered to become Jesus' disciples, but weren't ready to pay the price (Matthew 8:18-20, Luke 9:57-58).

One who did answer the call and was willing to pay the price was Matthew (Matthew 9:9, Mark 2:14, Luke 5:27-28). Jesus called Matthew after the incident when the paralytic was lowered through the roof. Matthew gave a feast for Jesus and the other disciples. Jesus used the occasion to teach a lesson about fasting.

Out of the many disciples whom Jesus had, He decided to select twelve of them for a special role and ministry. What was the purpose of choosing the twelve Apostles?

Mark 3:14-15 states three purposes:

1) that they might be with Him

> As Jesus' constant companions, the Apostles would know Him better than anyone. They would also become better acquainted with the teaching.

2) that He might send them out to preach

> Jesus needed to delegate responsibility to people He could trust. Also, He trained them to carry on His work by having them actually do the work.

3) to have authority to drive out demons

> Jesus not only taught the Apostles, He gave them the power they needed to do the work.

Acts 1:8 lists another very important role the Apostles were to play: They were to be witnesses. Because they were witnesses, John would later write, "That which was from the beginning, which we have heard, which we have seen with our eyes, which we have looked at and our hands have touched – this we proclaim concerning the Word of life." (1 John 1:1 NIV) It is the first-hand, eyewitness testimony of the Apostles which makes it possible for us, who are not eyewitnesses, to believe.

III.   The Message

What was the essence of Jesus' teaching?

> Matthew summarizes the message as, "...Repent for the kingdom of heaven is near." (Matthew 4:17 NIV) This is exactly the same message which John the Baptist had preached (Matthew 3:2).

However, Jesus did not stop with that short statement. He went on to tell people about the Kingdom of Heaven (or as the other accounts say, the Kingdom of God). He talked about the nature of it and the kind of people who belong to it. Shortly after Jesus chose the twelve, He gave what we call the 'Sermon on the Mount.' It might be better to call it the inauguration sermon, or the ordination sermon. Matthew, chapters 5 through 7 and Luke 6:20-49 summarize the sermon.

An outline of the major points in the sermon is:

> 1) The type of people in the Kingdom – the beatitudes (Matthew 5:3-12)
>
> 2) The responsibility of those in the Kingdom toward the world – salt and light (Matthew 5:13-16)
>
> 3) Jesus' teaching contrasted to the Law (Matthew 5:17-7:12)
>
> > a) Jesus came to fulfill, not abolish (Matthew 5:17-20)

Jesus emphasized that the Law would not disappear until everything was accomplished. That meant, of course, that when everything was accomplished, the Law would disappear. This is an extremely important concept to grasp. In Christ, the Law is fulfilled. It is no longer in force.

There are some who say that Jesus abolished the ceremonial portions of the Mosaic Law, but that the moral portions of the Law are still in force. The problem with this concept is that Scripture does not make a distinction between the ceremonial and moral. The Law is always regarded as a unity; a single entity. Jesus fulfilled, and therefore nullified the entire Law, not just a portion of it. The entire book of Galatians argues that the Law is no longer in force. Yes, this even includes the Ten Commandments. They are part of a system which has been done away with.

How can this be, since Jesus and the Apostles seem to endorse many of the concepts or principles of the Law, including the Ten Commandments? The answer is simple. The Mosaic Law originated with God. It reflects His personality. In the same way, the New Covenant also originated with God and reflects His personality. Since God's character does not change, it would be surprising if there were not points of similarity between the Old and New Covenants.

The point becomes clearer when we understand the purpose of the Mosaic Law. One of its purposes was to demonstrate that we are incapable of living up to the standard of perfection the Law demands. Therefore, it acted as a custodian or guide to lead us to Christ (Galatians 3:23-25). The other function of the Law is that it foreshadowed the New Covenant. As Paul wrote to the Colossians, "Therefore do not let anyone judge you by what you eat or drink, or with regard to a religious festival, a New Moon celebration or a Sabbath day. These are a shadow of the things that were to come; the reality, however, is found in Christ." (Colossians 2:16-17 NIV)

Many things in the Law served as a picture of spiritual realities in the New Covenant. For example, the Passover points to Christ's sacrifice. The same is true of some of the other sacrifices. The Tabernacle, and later the Temple, is a portrait of the church.

The basis of the Law was performance. "Moses describes in this way the righteousness that is by the law: "The man who does these things will live by them."" (Romans 10:5 NIV) Under the New Covenant in Christ, righteousness is obtained by faith, not by works. It is the attitude of the heart, not performance which God is looking for. To explain the difference in another way: In the New Covenant God is transforming us into the kind of people who don't need to be constrained by regulations – we do by nature what is right.

b) Specific examples of the difference in relationships between people (Matthew 5:21-48)

> Murder
>
> Adultery
>
> Divorce
>
> Oaths
>
> Retaliation
>
> Treatment of enemies

In each of these cases the focus is on the attitude which produces the act rather than the act itself.

c) Specific examples of the difference in the relationship to God (Matthew 6:1-34)

     Benevolence

     Prayer

     Fasting

     Priorities

     Practical application – physical needs, putting the Kingdom first

In these examples we see that our focus should not be on ourselves, but on God.

d) Specific examples of the difference in regard to oneself (Matthew 7:1-12)

     Judging

     Discernment

     Reliance on God rather than self

     The Golden Rule

4) Kingdom living (Matthew 7:13-27)

     a) Entering the Kingdom – it's not popular or easy

     b) Results of Kingdom living – good fruit

     c) Doing the will of God vs doing

     d) Putting Christ's words into practice

IV.   Under The Law Or In The Kingdom?

Unfortunately, there are many who call themselves Christians who are still trying to live by a system of law. To live by a code of behavior is not following Christ. Those who are in the Kingdom of Heaven are transformed from within. Their actions are not governed by an external code, but are the natural result of the good which is on the inside.

ം‌ഽഔ

A Spiritual Kingdom

Introduction: After Jesus selected the twelve Apostles, He changed the thrust of His ministry. Oh, He still went about doing miracles and healing people. He still spoke to the crowds and taught them. He still proclaimed the coming of the Kingdom. But there were also noticeable differences.

> 1) Before the Sermon on the Mount, Jesus called people to discipleship. While afterwards He still did so, the emphasis changed to training the twelve.

> 2) Before the Sermon on the Mount, Jesus had ministered only to people of Jewish descent. True, He had taught Samaritans in Sychar, but though they were half-breeds, they also traced their descent from the Jewish patriarchs. During this phase of Jesus' ministry, we get the first glimpses that His message was for Gentiles as well. The Kingdom of Heaven was for all people, not just for those of Jewish descent.

> 3) Jesus also changed His teaching method. After the Sermon on the Mount Jesus began to teach by using parables.

I.   A Centurion's Faith

It's ironic that one of the first people to really understand Jesus was a Gentile. When Jesus arrived back in Capernaum after giving the Sermon on the Mount, a delegation Jewish Elders approached Him on behalf of a Roman centurion. They asked Him to heal one of the man's servants. Jesus responded favorably to the request. But while He was on the way, the centurion sent more friends asking Jesus not to trouble Himself by coming in person. As a person under authority, the centurion recognized Jesus' authority to command – and be obeyed. Jesus was amazed at the man's faith and declared that He hadn't found that great a faith in Israel (Matthew 8:5-13, Luke 7:1-10). This was the first time anybody understood the implications of Jesus' ability to heal and perform miracles. Nicodemus had stated that the miracles were proof that God was with Jesus (John 3:2), but he didn't seem to grasp the next logical conclusion – that the miracles implied that God was not only with Jesus, but that Jesus had divine authority and was to be obeyed.

Not long after this, Jesus gave another proof of His authority. In the village of Nain, he raised the son of a widow woman from death. As a result of this incident the news of Jesus spread even further than it had before (Luke 7:11-17).

II.   John Doubts

While all this was going on, John the Baptist was languishing in prison. Herod Antipas (son of Herod the Great) had arrested John because John declared that Herod's marriage to Herodias (wife of Herod's brother, Philip) was unlawful (Matthew 14:3-5, Mark 6:17-18).

While in prison, John began to doubt. He heard about the things Jesus was doing, but began to wonder if Jesus was really the One who was to come. The accounts do not tell us why John began to doubt. It's possible that John had the same mistaken idea of the Messiah that many of the other Jews had – that the Messiah was going to be an earthly king who would drive the Romans out of Palestine and would restore the Kingdom of Israel. Jesus wasn't living up to this picture. His teaching and ministry seemed to be totally apolitical. The miracles certainly demonstrated that Jesus had authority, but He wasn't using that authority to confront the political powers. He hadn't even done anything to rescue John from his unjust imprisonment. In order to answer his doubts, John sent some of his disciples to Jesus to ask whether He really was the One they were looking for (Matthew 11:2-6, Luke 7:18-23). This was ironic because it was John who had identified Jesus as the One who was to come (John 1:29-34).

Instead of answering John directly, Jesus simply referred to the miracles He had been performing. Jesus' reply was an allusion to the Messianic prophecies of Isaiah. In other words, Jesus was doing the things which Isaiah prophesied the Messiah would do. (For example, see Isaiah 26:19, 29:18-19, 35:5-6, 61:1-2.) Jesus concluded His message by telling John, "Blessed is the man who does not fall away on account of me." (Matthew 11:6 NIV)

Lesson: When hard times come – and they will come – we should not question what God has made plain during the good times. The way to deal with doubts is to keep coming back to the facts – the raw data. When we stop and think it through, we understand that there is objective truth – truth which does not change according to circumstances.

Where do we find objective truth?

> It is in the Bible. While praying to God, Jesus declared, "… your word is truth." (John 17:17 NIV) Other passages in the New Testament also refer to the "word of truth" (Ephesians 1:13, Colossians 1:5, 2 Timothy 2:15, James 1:18). We can rely on the Bible because the things which we can verify and check out, invariably do check out. Since they do, we can have confidence that the things we can't check are accurate too.

After John's disciples left, Jesus spoke to the crowds about John (Matthew 11:7-19, Luke 7:24-35). He declared that John was the greatest of men. This must have been quite a shock to the Jews who gave that honor to the likes of Abraham, Moses and Elijah.

Jesus went on to say that the least in the Kingdom of Heaven is greater than John. How can this be?

> While John announced the coming of the Kingdom, he did not get to experience it. Those in the Kingdom have been given new life and the indwelling of the Holy Spirit. Please note that those who are in the Kingdom are not superior to John because of inherent greatness, but because of what has been imputed or given them. Those in the Kingdom are great because they are in Christ. Because they are in Christ, they get to share in His glory (for example, see John 17:22).

III.   Further Incidents

During this time several other incidents occurred which are worth mentioning.

> 1) During a dinner, a sinful woman anointed Jesus (Luke 7:36-50). Her actions were in stark contrast to the host who had failed to show Jesus even common courtesy. Jesus used the occasion to teach about forgiveness. We will demonstrate love in proportion to our recognition of what we have been forgiven. "…he who has been forgiven little loves little." (Luke 7:47 NIV)

> 2) Pharisees and teachers of the law accused Jesus of doing miracles by satanic power (Matthew 12:22-45, Mark 3:20-30). Jesus pointed out that this could not be true because it would mean that Satan was working against himself. Jesus went on to warn against the unforgivable sin – blasphemy against the Holy Spirit. Why is this sin unforgivable?

>> Because the Spirit works through our conscience. It is our conscience which convicts us of sin (Romans 2:13-15). If we destroy our conscience, it cannot convict us. (For example, compare 1 Corinthians 4:4, 1 Timothy 4:1-2.) If we are not conscious of sin, we won't repent of it. If we won't repent, we cannot be forgiven.

> 3) During this time Jesus' family concluded that He was crazy and tried to take custody of Him (Matthew 12:46-50, Mark 3:20-21, 31-35, Luke 8:19-21). As a result, Jesus declared that His true family are those who do God's will.

> 4) Jesus also performed many more miracles.

>> a) The stilling of a storm (Matthew 8:23-27, Mark 4:35-41, Luke 8:22-25).

>> b) Casting demons out of a man into swine (Matthew 8:28-34, Mark 5:1-20, Luke 8:26-39).

>> c) Healing two blind men (Matthew 9:27-31).

d) Casting the demon out of a deaf-mute (Matthew 9:32-34).

5) Jesus visited Nazareth one last time and was rejected again (Matthew 13:54-58, Mark 6:1-6).

6) After being rejected in Nazareth, Jesus made another preaching tour of Galilee (Matthew 9:35-38, Mark 6:6)

IV.   Teaching By Parable

One of the most striking characteristics of this phase of Jesus' ministry is that He began to use parables in His teaching.

What is a parable?

> It is a story of ordinary events or conditions which is used to make a spiritual point. They are not necessarily true in that they are about a specific incident which actually happened, but they do reflect common experiences or things which are known to occur. For example, when Jesus told the parable about the man who went out to sow his seed, He wasn't referring to a specific man on a particular farm. He was speaking in general terms. Similarly, when Jesus told the story about a man who found buried treasure, He probably didn't have a specific incident in mind. But we all know that people sometimes do find buried treasure.

Why did Jesus use parables?

> There probably were three reasons:
>
> 1) To conceal. In spite of all the miracles Jesus had shown, the hostility of the Scribes and Pharisees was increasing. Since they had already rejected the truth which was so plainly set before them, Jesus started using parables to preclude their understanding. Since they had hardened their hearts, God was going to use their hardened condition to bring about the fulfillment of the divine plan. Jesus quoted from Isaiah 6:9-10 to establish this very point (Matthew 13:11-15, Mark 4:11-12, Luke 8:10).

2) To reveal. In contrast to the attitude of the Jewish authorities, those who had a heart for the truth and doing God's will were able to perceive the meaning of the parables (Matthew 13:16-17).

3) Though the Gospels do not say so, one reason to use parables, no doubt, was because they are easy to remember.

There are three major groups of parables. In this first group (Matthew 13:1-53, Mark 4:1-34, Luke 8:4-18) are:

1) The sower

2) The weeds

3) The hidden treasure

4) The costly pearl

5) The net

6) The lamp on a stand

7) Seeds growing

8) The mustard seed

V.   Letting Go (sending out the 12)

During this period of His ministry, Jesus made training the twelve Apostles a priority. In addition to teaching them about the Kingdom, Jesus seems to have followed a deliberate method to prepare the Apostles for the role they would fill.

1) He began with prayer. Jesus instructed the Apostles to pray for workers who could meet the needs of the crowds they encountered everywhere on their travels (Matthew 9:35-38). It is highly significant that the Apostles became the answer to their own prayers. Right after Jesus told them to pray for workers, He sent them out to work.

Lesson: When we pray, we need to do so with hearts that are willing to act to fulfill the prayer.

2) Jesus equipped them to do the work. Jesus not only told them to do it, He gave them the power and authority to do it (Matthew 10:1, Mark 6:7, Luke 9:1).

3) Jesus gave them specific instructions about how they were to do the work (Matthew 10:5-11:1, Mark 6:8-11, Luke 9:2-5).

4) He gave them the support they needed. He sent them out in teams of two.

5) He trusted them to do the work. He didn't hover over them and second-guess what they did. He stayed behind while they went out.

VI.   Feeding The 5,000

Upon the Apostles' return from their ministry tours, Jesus decided to take them to the other side of the lake for some quiet time by themselves. There were several reasons for this.

1) He and the Apostles were tired. They had worked hard and had just returned from a tour. They had been so busy that at times they hadn't even had time to eat (Mark 6:31).

2) They were in sorrow. They had just received word that John the Baptist had been executed (Matthew 14:13).

3) Herod Antipas, who had beheaded John, was attempting to see Jesus (Luke 9:9). Understandably, Jesus had no desire to see him. The day would come when Jesus would stand before Herod, but this wasn't the right time.

The trip didn't quite work out as Jesus intended. The crowd figured out where they were going and got there ahead of them. In spite of being tired and in sorrow, Jesus had compassion on the crowd and taught them. The next day they moved on down the coast and the crowd again followed. Since the crowd had no way of getting food, Jesus fed them (Matthew 14:13-21, Mark 6:30-44, Luke 9:10-17, John 6:1-15).

Aside from the resurrection, the feeding of the 5,000 is the only miracle which all four of the Gospel accounts record. While a notable miracle in itself, this incident was significant in another way. It was the background for one of the most important turning points in Jesus' ministry.

The people decided to make Jesus, king – by force, if necessary. Jesus managed to send the Apostles away, forestall the crowd and dismiss them. He, then, walked on the surface of the lake to the boat where the Apostles were trying to row to their destination against a strong headwind. When they reached the shore, the news spread that Jesus had returned and people mobbed Him as before. Meanwhile the crowd which Jesus had left on the opposite side of the lake managed to cross. They came looking for Jesus, still bent on making Him king.

VII.   Physical Or Heavenly Bread?

The crowd caught up with Jesus at the synagogue at Capernaum. There Jesus preached His sermon on the Bread of Life (John 6:22-71). The people asked Jesus to provide them 'bread from heaven', thinking of physical bread, or the manna which the Israelites had eaten during their wanderings in the wilderness. But the crowd misunderstood the real meaning of the manna. According to Deuteronomy 8:3, the manna was really a symbol for God's word. It is not the physical bread, but God's living Word which gives life. Jesus tried to explain that He was that living Word which had come down from heaven.

The crowd would not accept Jesus' explanations. They wanted a free lunch. When Jesus would not provide it; when He would not cater to their 'felt needs', they became disgruntled and left. "From this time many of his disciples turned back and no longer followed him." (John 6:66 NIV)

This was a turning point in Jesus' ministry. It was the end of His popularity. The crowds would never be quite as large again. They wanted physical bread and were not interested in the spiritual food Jesus provided. From now on the opposition would build until it took Jesus to the cross.

VIII.   Making A Choice

Where does this leave us? What are we looking for? Do we follow Jesus in the hope of obtaining physical blessings? Or are we looking for the true bread from heaven?

 ଽଠଓ

Ministry in the Face of Opposition

Introduction: The feeding of the 5,000 and the sermon on the Bread of Life were a major turning point in Jesus' ministry. Jesus made it clear that He would not cater to the 'felt needs' of the people. His Kingdom was a spiritual one. Because Jesus refused to meet the material expectations of the crowd, John 6:66 says, "From this time many of his disciples turned back and no longer followed him." (NIV)

After this two changes were noticeable:

> 1) Jesus had already encountered conflict with, and rejection by, the Jewish authorities from Judea. Now He began to experience opposition in Galilee as well. Not only the leaders, but the common people, showed hostility to Him. Yes, crowds still gathered around for healing. Yes, Jesus would address crowds of up to 4,000 people. Yes, Jesus still had at least 72 disciples whom He could send out on an evangelistic tour. Yes, Jesus still characterized the harvest as plentiful (Luke 10:2). But it wasn't the same. Whereas before, Jesus was welcomed almost everywhere in Galilee, now there were towns where He wasn't welcome (Luke 10:10).

> 2) Another major change is that Jesus started to distance Himself from Galilee. During the next phase of His ministry, Jesus spent quite a bit of time in areas outside of Galilee.

I.   Respite From Controversy

Not long after the sermon on the Bread of Life, Jesus had a run-in with some religious leaders who had come up to Galilee from Jerusalem (Matthew 15:1-20, Mark 7:1-23). They were upset that Jesus' disciples didn't observe ritual washing before eating. Jesus used their objection to teach about internal versus external righteousness. In a way, this was a continuation of the subject of the sermon on the Bread of Life. The people wanted physical bread, Jesus tried to give them spiritual food. The leaders from Jerusalem thought it was important to look religious; Jesus taught that it was more important to have a righteous character. Right actions will be the natural result of a heart that is right.

Right after this incident, Jesus left Galilee and traveled north to the region of Tyre and Sidon (Matthew 15:21-28, Mark 7:24-30). This was territory which had never been a part of Israel. Instead it belonged to Phoenicia. Aside from the time Jesus spent in Egypt as an infant, this was the only time He traveled to any place outside of the boundaries of ancient Israel.

We aren't told why Jesus decided to go there. One reason may have been to get away from controversy for a while. After dashing the hopes of the crowd and exposing the hypocrisy of their religious leaders, Jesus may have wanted to give people some time to cool off. So, He removed Himself from the area.

Another reason to leave Galilee and go to foreign parts was simply to get some rest. Remember that before the feeding of the 5,000, Jesus and His disciples had crossed the Sea of Galilee in order to get some rest. They hadn't gotten any because the crowds arrived at the place where they were going, first. Then, upon their return after a sleepless night, they had been inundated by another needy crowd. This was followed by the stress of the controversy over the sermon on the Bread of Life. Jesus and His disciples must have been exhausted. They needed to get away. Mark writes that on this journey Jesus did not want anyone to know were He was staying (Mark 7:24).

The news got out anyway, and it wasn't long before a Canaanite woman began pestering Jesus to heal her daughter. One of the interesting things about this encounter is that the woman had a better understanding of who Jesus was than many of the Jews (Matthew 15:22). At first, Jesus ignored the woman's request. When the disciples wearied of her persistence, however, Jesus responded that His mission was only to "the lost sheep of Israel". Changing metaphors He said it wouldn't be right to take what belonged to the children and toss it to the dog (Matthew 15:24-26 Mark 7:27). Far from becoming upset at her place in the metaphor, the woman pointed out that even dogs have some rights. Because of her answer and the faith which prompted it, Jesus healed her daughter (Matthew 15:28, Mark 7:29).

> **Tangent:** Why would Jesus respond in such an insensitive and rude way (inferring that she was a dog) to a woman who asked for help?
>
> Jesus was not expressing His own attitude but confronting the disciples with their prejudices. In their minds, because the Canaanite woman was a Gentile, she was unclean and was inferior to those of Jewish descent. Jesus, on the other hand, responded to faith wherever, and in whomever, He found it. After all, John had proclaimed that Jesus was the lamb which takes away the sin of the world (John 1:29), not just that of the Israelites. It would take a long time for the disciples to grasp the fact that Jesus' mission and salvation is for everyone.
>
> Why, then, did Jesus say He was sent to the lost sheep of Israel? Because in God's scheme of things, even though He was bringing salvation to the whole world, salvation was going to come through the Jews. Paul writes, "I am not ashamed of the gospel, because it is the power of God for the salvation of everyone who believes: first for the Jew, then for the Gentile." (Romans 1:16 NIV)

After returning from Phoenicia, Jesus traveled to the region southeast of the Sea of Galilee – the Decapolis (named so because it contained ten cities) (Mark 7:31-37). While there, Jesus healed many people (Matthew 15:29-31). One of the most notable miracles was a reprise of the feeding of the 5,000. This time 4,000 ate (Matthew 15:32-39, Mark 8:1-13), and the miracle exposed the same kind of spiritual hardness of heart as the earlier feeding had.

II.   Signs

When Jesus went to the Galilean side of the lake after feeding the 4,000, some Pharisees and Sadducees accosted Him and demanded that He show them a sign from heaven (Matthew 16:1-4, Mark 8:11-13). What sort of sign they expected Jesus to show them is difficult to say. What more could Jesus show them to authenticate His message than He had already done? Since they refused to believe the signs Jesus had already given, He told them that the only other sign which would be given was the sign of Jonah. This was an obvious reference to Jesus' coming death and resurrection. If the resurrection is not enough to convince someone of who Jesus is, then nothing will.

After this encounter, Jesus traveled to the eastern shore of the lake again. On this journey Jesus warned the 12 against the teaching of the Pharisees and Sadducees.

Jesus took the 12 and traveled north to the region of Caesarea Philippi. On the way, Jesus healed a blind man at Bethsaida (Mark 8:22-26). When they arrived at their destination, Jesus asked the Apostles who the people were saying that He was (Matthew 16:13-20, Mark 8:27-30, Luke 9:18-21). After receiving various replies, Jesus asked the Apostles who they thought He was. Peter replied with one of the two basic creedal statements of the Christian faith. What was it?

> "…You are the Christ, the Son of the living God."
> (Matthew 16:16 NIV)

This statement is so fundamental that Jesus said He would build His church upon the truth it expresses.

Lesson: Any church which does not acknowledge these basic facts about who Jesus is, is not the Lord's church. Many of the heresies which have arisen over the years deny one or more of the truths expressed in Peter's confession. For example, Islam calls Jesus the Christ (although Muslims have no understanding of what His being Christ means), but deny that He is the Son of God. Therefore, since Jesus declared that He would build His church on the truth which Peter confessed, we can be sure that Dar-ul-Islam (the house of Islam) is not part of the Lord's church.

> **Tangent:** A full explanation of Peter's confession is well beyond the scope of this study. Briefly, when we call Jesus the Christ (or Messiah) we mean that He is our Prophet. It is He who brings us God's message. Anyone who brings a

message which contradicts what Jesus said, is not of God. As Christ, Jesus is also our Priest. He intercedes for us before God. He also offered the perfect sacrifice for sin which enables us to become holy in God's sight. As Christ, Jesus is also our King. We owe Him our allegiance and obedience. He not only rules over us, but protects us from our enemies – including death. When we call Jesus, God's Son, we proclaim Him to be God in human flesh.

Tangent: In addition to Peter's confession, what is the other basic creedal statement of the Christian faith?

"…Christ died for our sins according to the
Scriptures, that he was buried, that he was raised on
the third day according to the Scriptures,"
(1 Corinthians 15:3-4 NIV)

This statement is the Gospel (the Good News) in it's most basic form. Peter's confession expresses the truth about who Jesus is. The Gospel tells us what Jesus did. An understanding of the truths in both statements is crucial. Again, a full explanation is far beyond the scope of this study. In brief, the work of Christ fulfilled, and was in harmony with, the Scriptures. There was a specific purpose in Jesus' death. It satisfied God's justice which demands that sin be punished. Jesus not only died and was buried, He rose again – demonstrating that He has conquered death. His victory gives us hope.

Though Peter had grasped the essential truth of who Jesus was, he and the other Apostles did not yet understand Jesus' mission. From this time on Jesus began to explain the coming crucifixion and resurrection (Matthew 16:21, Mark 8:31, Luke 9:22). The idea that Jesus was going to die was too much for Peter to comprehend and accept. He rebuked Jesus for saying such things and was severely reprimanded for his rebuke (Matthew 16:22-23, Mark 8:32-33).

This led to a lesson on the cost of following Jesus. Jesus was headed for the cross. A disciple must pick up his own cross and follow (Matthew 16:24-28, Mark 8:34-9:1, Luke 9:23-27). Following Jesus not only means being willing to die for Him but, more importantly, it means dying to self in order to do His will.

Right after this something occurred which would have qualified as one of those signs the Pharisees and Sadducees were demanding. Jesus took three of the Apostles up on a mountain and was transfigured in their presence (Matthew 17:1-13, Mark 9:2-13, Luke 9:28-36). They got to see a glimpse of Jesus' heavenly glory. Not only that, Moses and Elijah (the two prophets the Jews revered the most) appeared and talked with Jesus about His approaching death in Jerusalem. However, the high point of the entire experience was a voice from heaven declaring Jesus as the beloved Son.

Coming down from the mountain, Jesus healed a demon possessed boy (Matthew 17:14-21, Mark 9:14-29, Luke 9:37-43). Then, He and the Apostles traveled to Galilee. On the way, Jesus again warned them about His coming death and resurrection (Matthew 17:22-23, Mark 9:30-32, Luke 9:43-45).

In spite of Jesus' teaching about the need to deny self, the Apostles still didn't get it. They were concerned about who would be the greatest. So, Jesus had to give them another lesson about humility and forgiveness – this time using a child as an illustration to make His point (Matthew 18:1-35, Mark 9:33-50, Luke 9:46-50).

Then Jesus left Galilee for the last time before His death (Matthew 19:1, Mark 10:1, Luke 9:51).

III.   Back To Judea

Jesus had deliberately avoided Judea because the Jewish authorities were planning to kill Him (John 7:1). Now, however, Jesus decided to attend the Feast of Tabernacles (John 7:2-10). God's time had come for Jesus to move into the final phase of His ministry.

It is from this period – the last six months or so of Jesus' life – that, aside from the Sermon on Mount, we have the largest collection of Jesus' teaching. Much of this teaching was not in the form of prepared lessons, but grew out of the opportunity provided by specific incidents.

1) The water of life, during the Feast of Tabernacles (John 7:14-44).

2) Justice – the woman caught in adultery (John 8:2-11).

3) The light of the world (John 8:12-30).

4) The true children of Abraham, and the children of the devil (John 8:31-47).

5) Jesus' identity – the 'I Am' (John 8:48-59).

6) Spiritual blindness (John 9:1-41).

7) What is important, during a visit to the home of Mary and Martha (Luke 10:38-42).

8) About prayer (Luke 11:1-13).

9) About evil spirits, upon being accused of casting out demons by demonic power (Luke 11:14-26).

10) Who is Blessed (Luke 11:27-28).

11) The sign of Jonah (Luke 11:29-32).

12) Light and darkness (Luke 11:33-36).

13) Woes pronounced on hypocrisy, while dining at a Pharisees' house (Luke 11:37-54).

14) Concerning hypocrisy, and faithfulness under persecution (Luke 12:1-12).

15) Concerning worry, and God's provision of the necessities of life (Luke 12:22-34).

16) Watchfulness (Luke 12:35-48).

17) Division and reconciliation (Luke 12:49-59).

18) The need for repentance (Luke 13:1-5).

19) Who will be saved (Luke 13:22-30).

20) What is lawful on the Sabbath (Luke (14:1-6).

21) Humility (Luke 14:7-14).

22) The cost of discipleship (Luke 14:25-35).

23) The coming of the Kingdom (Luke 17:20-37).

It is also from this time that we have the second group of parables.

1) The good shepherd (John 10:1-21).

2) The good Samaritan (Luke 10:25-37).

3) The rich fool (Luke 12:13-21).

4) The mustard seed and yeast (Luke 13:18-21).

5) The great banquet (Luke 14:15-24).

6) The lost sheep (Luke 15:1-7).

7) The lost coin (Luke 15:8-10).

8) The lost son (Luke 15:11-32).

9) The unrighteous steward (Luke 16:1-15).

10) The rich man and Lazarus (Luke 16:19-31).

11) The widow and the judge (Luke 18:1-8).

12) The Pharisee and the tax collector (Luke 18:9-14).

13) The ten investors (Luke 19:11-27).

IV.   Prelude To The End

Controversy and confrontation with the Jewish authorities marked Jesus' time in Judea. Though Jesus was able to send out 72 disciples as advance men to prepare the way for Him, and they had success, it was in an environment of rejection and opposition (Luke 10:1-24). Shortly after the 72 returned and reported to Jesus, He left Judea and crossed the Jordan River into Perea (John 10:40-42). There, in contrast to the Jewish authorities in Judea, many believed.

What prompted Jesus to leave Perea and return to Judea was the death of Lazarus (John 11:1-16). Raising Lazarus from the dead brought the clash with the Jewish authorities to a head. "...Here is this man performing many miraculous signs. If we let him go on like this, everyone will believe in him, and then the Romans will come and take away both our place and our nation." (John 11:47-48 NIV) It's ironic that the very people who had earlier demanded a sign from Jesus, now admitted that He had already performed many signs. Because of their own selfish ambitions, rather than accept the signs, the authorities decided they had to do away with Jesus. "So from that day on they plotted to take his life." (John 11:53 NIV) This wasn't the first time the authorities had decided to kill Jesus. But now they started to take serious action. This time they would carry out the threat.

However, the time was not yet right for Jesus to offer Himself as the perfect sin offering, so He withdrew to a small village near the desert (John 11:54) until just before the Passover feast. Six days before the Passover, Jesus arrived at Bethany (John 12:1). There, at a feast given in His honor, Mary anointed Jesus with costly perfume (Matthew 26:6-13, Mark 14:3-9, John 12:1-11). When the disciples objected, Jesus stated that what Mary had done was in preparation for His burial.

The stage was now set for the final week of Jesus' ministry on earth. During this week the most momentous event in human history would take place.

V.   Accept Or Reject?

Where does this leave us? Are we willing to make the same confession as Peter did about who Jesus is, or will we follow the lead of the Jewish authorities who rejected Him in spite of the undeniable signs He performed? Will we honor Jesus like Mary did, or will we put self-interest first?

&)(&

62

The Final Week

Introduction: The Gospel writers devote more space to the final week of Jesus' ministry, and particularly the crucifixion, than to any other portion of His life. All of human history, and God's plan to reconcile mankind to Himself, pivot around these events. The death, burial and resurrection of Christ are the most important events which have ever taken place.

I.   Sunday – The King Comes (Matthew 21:1-11, Mark 11:1-11, Luke 19:29-44, John 12:12-19)

Jesus spent a quiet Sabbath, that is Saturday, in Bethany – presumably at the home of Martha, Mary and Lazarus. A large crowd found out that Jesus was there. They were curious to see Him and also Lazarus, whom Jesus had raised from the dead. The crowd's curiosity would have been frustrated by the restrictions on traveling on the Sabbath. But the ban was not in force on Sunday morning and when Jesus set out for Jerusalem, an enthusiastic mob of people greeted Him.

The news that Jesus was coming quickly spread and a second crowd from Jerusalem came to welcome Him. These two crowds escorted Jesus to Jerusalem.

Throughout His ministry Jesus had proclaimed the coming of the Kingdom of God. He had also demonstrated His divine authority time after time. The crowds recognized and welcomed Him as their King or Messiah. They waved palm branches which were a sign of Jewish nationalism. They also started shouting a quote from Psalm 118, "Blessed is he who comes in the name of the Lord!" and other nationalistic slogans.

Jesus was being proclaimed King, but what kind of Kingdom was He the King of? Jesus gave a very clear indication of the nature of His Kingdom by riding into Jerusalem on a donkey. What did the symbolism point to?

> Jesus' riding a donkey into Jerusalem was a fulfillment of Zechariah 9:9-10. That passage says that the King will

proclaim peace to the nations. Jesus came not to conquer, but
to proclaim peace. Jesus once explained that the Kingdom of
God was not a political entity, but is something which is
internal (Luke 17:20-21). This was a very different concept
than that of the Jewish nationalists. It may help to explain
why some of these same people who greeted Jesus so enthu-
siastically turned on Him just a few days later.

After looking around the Temple, Jesus left Jerusalem and returned
to Bethany.

II.   Monday – Demonstration Of Authority (Matthew 21:12-
19, Mark 11:12-19, Luke 19:45-48)

On Monday morning, Jesus returned to Jerusalem. On the way He
cursed a fig tree. Why did He do so?

Judging by its appearance, there should have been figs on the
tree. There weren't. Jesus used the tree as an illustration or a
parable of the power of faith. On the one hand, faith produces
action. On the other, lack of faith results in being cursed. It is
probable that Jesus was referring to the Jewish people as the
fig tree. Their lack of faith in rejecting Christ, resulted in
destruction.

Upon arriving at Jerusalem, Jesus cleansed the Temple a second time
– just as He had done two years earlier.

III.   Tuesday – A Day Of Confrontation

Tuesday was an incredibly busy day. On the way into Jerusalem,
Jesus taught the disciples the lesson of the fig tree. When He arrived
at the Temple, the priests and elders questioned His authority to do
what He was doing – presumably in reference to His cleansing the
Temple (Matthew 21:23-27, Mark 11:27-33, Luke 20:1-8). Jesus
responded with a question about whether John's baptism was from
God or not.

Then Jesus told three parables for the benefit of those who had
challenged Him, warning them that they were in danger of not
entering the Kingdom of God. These were:

1) The parable of the two sons (Matthew 21:28-32).

2) The parable of the wicked tenants (Matthew 21:33-46, Mark 12:1-12, Luke 20:9-19).

3) The parable of the wedding feast (Matthew 22:1-14).

Next came questions designed to test Jesus.

1) The Pharisees tried to trap Him by asking whether it was right to pay taxes (Matthew 22:15-22, Mark 12:13-17, Luke 20:20-26).

2) No sooner had Jesus disposed of that problem when the Sadducees tried to stump Him with a question about the resurrection (Matthew 22:23-33, Mark 12:18-27, Luke 20:27-40).

3) After Jesus routed the Sadducees, a lawyer asked about the greatest commandment in the Law (Matthew 22:34-40, Mark 12:28-34).

After answering the lawyer, Jesus turned the tables on His questioners and asked them a question about the identity of David's son (Matthew 22:41-46, Mark 12:35-37, Luke 20:41-44). When they could not answer, Jesus proceeded to proclaim seven woes on the teachers of the Law and the Pharisees (Matthew 23:1-39, Mark 12:38-40, Luke 20:45-47).

Next, the scene shifts to the place where the offerings were collected. After Jesus observed a widow putting in two small coins, He proclaimed that she had put in more than all the rich people (Mark 12:41-44, Luke 21:1-4).

It was probably after this incident that a delegation of Greeks approached Jesus (John 12:20-36). We are not told what they proposed, but from Jesus' reaction it is likely that they offered Him the opportunity to come and teach among them. In other words, they offered Jesus a way to avoid the cross. Aside from the temptation immediately after His baptism, this was probably the most serious temptation Jesus ever faced. Upon making His choice to go through with the crucifixion, a voice from heaven again validated Jesus (John 12:27-28).

This day concluded Jesus' public ministry.

As Jesus and His disciples were leaving the Temple, Jesus predicted its destruction. When they reached the Mount of Olives, the disciples asked when this destruction would occur, and about the signs of Christ's coming and the end of the age (Matthew 24:1-25:16, Mark 13:1-37, Luke 21:5-36).

As part of His answer, Jesus told the parables of:

> 1) The ten virgins (Matthew 25:1-13).
>
> 2) The ten talents (Matthew 25:14-30).
>
> 3) The sheep and the goats (Matthew 25:31-46).

IV.   Wednesday – A Day Of Rest

We don't have a record of any specific actions or teachings by Jesus on this day. However, it is very likely the day the religious leaders met at the home of the High Priest in order to finalize their plans to kill Jesus (Matthew 26:3-5, Mark 14:1-2, Luke 22:1-2).

As treasurer, it's likely that Judas was sent to buy the Passover lamb on this day. He used the opportunity, when he was away from the scrutiny of the other disciples, to sell Jesus for 30 pieces of silver (Matthew 26:14-16, Mark 14:10-11, Luke 22:3-6).

V.   Thursday – Preparation

On Thursday, Jesus sent Peter and John into Jerusalem to prepare for the Passover meal (Matthew 26:17-19, Mark 14:12-16, Luke 22:7-13). They inspected the room where the meal would take place. Then, they took the lamb to the Temple, to sacrifice it. After slaughtering the lamb, they returned to the house and roasted it.

After finishing the preparations, Peter and John apparently returned to Bethany and conducted Jesus and the others back to the upper room (Mark 14:17).

Luke records that the disciples had another squabble about who was the greatest (Luke 22:24-27). Luke doesn't tell us when the dispute took place that night, but it is logical to assume that it happened as they were gathering around the table. Who would get the places of honor next to Jesus?

It was probably in response to this squabble that Jesus taught the disciples a lesson in humility and service by washing their feet (John 13:1-20).

Shortly after Jesus washed the disciples' feet, He predicted that one of them would betray Him. Peter signaled John to ask Jesus who it was. Jesus replied that it was the one to whom He would give a piece of bread after dipping it in the dish. For a host to take a bit of food from the common dish with a piece of bread and present it to one of the guests was a means of displaying honor and courtesy to that guest. It's possible that during the course of the meal Jesus presented tidbits of food to several of the disciples. In any case, Jesus' offering the bread to Judas didn't seem to raise any questions in the minds of the other disciples.

Jesus presented Judas a choice along with the bread. "Who are you going to honor, Judas? Who are you going to put first? Yourself, or me?" By taking the bread, Judas chose self-interest and self-gratification over Jesus.

Once Judas made the choice, Jesus told him to carry out his plan quickly. Judas left the meal and went out to complete his dirty work (John 13:21-30).

It was probably after Judas left that Jesus instituted the Memorial meal which we call Communion. "…he took bread, gave thanks and broke it, and gave it to them, saying, "This is my body given for you; do this in remembrance of me."" (Luke 22:19 NIV) By means of the bread, Jesus identified Himself as the Passover sacrifice – the sacrifice of deliverance. (See 1 Corinthians 5:7-8, 1 Peter 1:18-19.)

"In the same way, after the supper he took the cup, saying, "This cup is the new covenant in my blood, which is poured out for you."" (Luke 22:20 NIV) Just as the Old Covenant had been sealed and ratified by blood (Exodus 24:5-8), Jesus' blood would usher in the

New Covenant prophesied by Jeremiah and Zechariah (Jeremiah 31:31-34, Zechariah 9:9-11, Hebrews 10:1-25).

After inaugurating the Memorial meal, which clearly pointed to His death and atoning sacrifice, Jesus explicitly told the disciples that He was going away (John 13:33). It was in this context Jesus predicted that Peter would deny Him (Matthew 26:34, Mark 14:30, Luke 22:34, John 13:38). Peter, of course, maintained that he was willing to give his life for Jesus. We tend to be rather hard on Peter because he failed. But it's worth keeping in mind that the rest of the disciples made the same profession of loyalty (Matthew 26:35, Mark 14:31).

Then, Jesus proceeded to give the disciples His final teachings before the crucifixion:

1) The way to the Father (John 14:1-14).

2) Promise of the Holy Spirit (John 14:15-31).

3) The Vine and the Branches (John 15:1-17).

4) Suffering for being a disciple (John 15:18-16:4).

5) The work of the Holy Spirit (John 16:5-16).

6) Their grief would turn to joy (John 16:17-33).

After giving these teachings, and before leaving the upper room, Jesus prayed. The first part of His prayer was for Himself (John 17:1-5). He, then, prayed for His disciples (John 17:6-19). He concluded by praying for all who would come to believe on Him (John 17:20-26).

VI.   Friday – Sacrifice

After leaving the upper room, Jesus and the disciples went to the Garden of Gethsemane. There Jesus prayed to be released from the necessity to go to the cross. Nevertheless, He accepted God's will (Matthew 26:36-42, Mark 14:32-36, Luke 22:41-42).

Just as He was done praying, Judas came to the garden leading a large group of armed men. He betrayed Jesus to them with a kiss (Matthew 26:47-50, Mark 14:43-46, Luke 22:47-48, John 18:2-3).

As Jesus had predicted (Matthew 26:31, Mark 14:27), all the disciples deserted Him (Matthew 26:56, Mark 14:50). Peter and John followed those who had arrested Jesus at a distance (John 18:15).

Jesus went through 6 hearings or trials. In order to harmonize the accounts of the trials and crucifixion, it's necessary to understand that Matthew, Mark and Luke write according to Jewish time reckoning. John writes using Roman time. Otherwise, the accounts seem to contradict one another – Jesus being crucified before sentence is pronounced on Him.

A. Religious

1) Before Annas – the former High Priest (John 18:13-24). Though the Romans had deposed Annas many, if not most, of the Jews still regarded him as the legitimate High Priest. Annas questioned Jesus about His disciples and His teaching. While this was going on, Peter and John gained access to the High Priest's courtyard. When asked if he was one of Jesus' disciples, Peter denied it.

2) Before Caiaphas – Annas' son-in-law (Matthew 26:57-68, Mark 14:53-65, Luke 22:54). Caiaphas was the nominal High Priest installed by the Romans. Because of his position as High Priest, he was also the head of the Sanhedrin, or supreme court of Israel. During this phase of the trial, the court produced false witnesses to testify against Jesus. Finally, Caiaphas asked Jesus point-blank whether He was the Christ. Jesus confessed that He was. The court, then, convicted Him of blasphemy, judged Him worthy of death and mocked Him. During this trial Peter denied Jesus a second and third time.

3) Before the full Sanhedrin (Matthew 27:1, Mark 15:1a, Luke 22:66-71). While before the full court, Jesus confessed to being the Son of God. Upon hearing this, the whole council condemned Him to

death for blasphemy and remanded Him to the Roman governor.

When Judas heard that Jesus had been condemned to death, he tried to return the money he had gotten to betray Jesus. Then he went out and hanged himself (Matthew 27:3-10).

B. Civil

4) Before Pilate – the Roman governor (Matthew 27:2, 11-14, Mark 15:1b-5, Luke 23:1-5, John 18:28-38). The Jews did not have the authority to put anyone to death, so they had to turn Jesus' case over to the Romans. However, they had a problem. The Roman governor would certainly not put a man to death on a charge that had to do with the Jewish religion. In order to get Pilate to hear the case, the Jewish authorities had to concoct a charge that was serious to the Romans. They chose two – sedition and pretensions of being king. Pilate quickly saw through these charges and tried to dismiss the case. When the Jews kept applying pressure, Pilate tried to sidestep on grounds of jurisdiction. He sent Jesus to Herod.

5) Before Herod – the ruler of Galilee (Luke 23:6-12). Jesus had nothing to say to the man who had murdered John, had no interest in the truth and merely wanted to see something sensational. After getting nothing from Jesus, Herod mocked Him and sent Him back to Pilate.

6) Before Pilate again (Matthew 27:15-26, Mark 15:6-15, Luke 23:13-25, John 18:39-19:16). During this phase, Pilate made two attempts to dismiss the case against Jesus. First, instead of releasing a prisoner of the people's choice, as was the custom at Passover, Pilate gave them the option of Jesus or a notorious criminal. He must have been dumbfounded when the Jews picked Barabbas. Next, Pilate tried to

let Jesus off with a lesser sentence – whipping instead of crucifixion. The crowd wouldn't have it. They demanded the death sentence even after Jesus was flogged.

One of the puzzling things about this whole scenario is why Pilate didn't show more backbone. He obviously knew that Jesus was innocent. He had the power to release Him. He had the Roman army at his back. Why didn't Pilate just tell the Jewish authorities where to get off?

> The key to the mystery seems to be the implied threat when the Jewish authorities said that the person who set Jesus free was not Caesar's friend (John 19:12). Pilate was already on political thin ice. He had been appointed governor by Sejanus, an advisor to Tiberius Caesar. Sejanus, however, was convicted of treason and executed shortly before Jesus came before Pilate. Therefore, any accusation of unreliability or disloyalty against Pilate would have had credibility in Rome. Therefore, Pilate had to either condemn Jesus, or risk his own neck. He chose expediency over honesty and justice.

Jesus was crucified at about 9 in the morning (Mark 15:25). He hung there for about 6 hours (Mark 15:34). In spite of His agony, it is amazing how focused on others Jesus was during those 6 hours. Of the 7 things Jesus said from the cross, 3 of them had to do with the wellbeing of other people.

1) "Father forgive them" (Luke 23:34).

2) "Today you shall be with me in Paradise" (Luke 23:43).

3) "Here is your mother" (John 19:26-27).

Jesus' other concern was to do the Father's will and to fulfill the prophecies about Himself.

4) "Why have you forsaken me?" (Mathew 27:46, Mark 15:34, in fulfillment of Psalm 22).

5) "I thirst" (John 19:28, to fulfill Scripture).

6) "It is finished" (John 19:30).

7) "Into your hands I commit my spirit" (Luke 23:46).

Darkness covered the land for about the last 3 hours Jesus hung on the cross (Mark 15:33). At the moment of His death, the curtain which separated the Holy Place from the Most Holy Place in the Temple was torn in two. This signified that the way to heaven was now open (Hebrews 10:19-20). There was an earthquake and many righteous people were raised to life. (Matthew 27:50-53, Mark 15:38, Luke 23:45).

One of the Roman soldiers made sure Jesus was dead by thrusting a spear into His side. Then, Joseph of Arimathea and Nicodemas took Jesus down from the cross and buried Him in a new tomb which belonged to Joseph (Matthew 27:57-61, Mark 15:42-47, Luke 23:50-56, John 19:31-42).

Then the enemies of Jesus made one of the biggest mistakes possible. They requested and got a Roman guard to protect the tomb (Matthew 27:62-66).

VII.   Victory Over The Odds

On the third day, that is the first day of the week (Sunday), people found the tomb empty. That it was empty is not in dispute. There are several theories to account for it being empty.

1) Swoon theory. Jesus somehow revived and made His way out of the tomb.

2) The wrong tomb theory. The disciples somehow got confused and went to the wrong place when they tried to finish the burial rites.

3) Fraud. The disciples stole the body (Matthew 28:11-15).

4) Visions and development of a legend. The disciples had dreams or visions in which they saw Jesus alive. They projected these visions back into history as a resurrection story.

5) Jesus rose from the dead.

Of all these theories, only the actual, bodily resurrection of the Christ can account for the facts. One of the most persuasive bits of evidence is that none of the disciples expected Jesus to rise. Yet, just 50 days after the crucifixion, these same men who ran away and denied that they even knew Jesus, boldly proclaimed Him. They didn't hesitate to condemn those who had killed Jesus. They went on to give their lives to proclaim the good news that Jesus had died and risen from the dead. The only thing which can account for the remarkable change in these men is if the resurrection is true.

VIII.   Truth Or Fiction?

The death, burial and resurrection of Christ are the fundamental doctrines of the Gospel. If the resurrection did not take place, then Christianity is false and all those who place their faith in Christ are deluded. If the resurrection did not take place, there is no forgiveness of sins (1 Corinthians 15:14-18). Do we believe?

೮೦೦೮

50 Days

Introduction: One of the most difficult things to do is to change a preconceived idea or concept by which we have governed our lives. To admit that the idea is wrong removes the foundation from under us.

Jesus' death was a profound shock to the disciples. In spite of the fact that Jesus had warned them ahead of time, the death did not fit into their notions of who the Messiah was or His mission. When Jesus died, their hopes died with Him.

A second shock to the disciples was to realize that Jesus rose from the grave. It spite of Jesus' explicit teaching about His death and resurrection, nobody expected Him to rise.

The 50 days following the crucifixion was a time of profound realignment in the disciples' understanding and of their priorities.

I.   A Series Of Sightings

When the women went to the tomb to finish the burial rituals they had not had time to complete on Friday, they found the tomb open and empty (Matthew 28:1-4, Mark 16:1-4, Luke 24:1-2, John 20:1). Mary Magdalene told Peter and John what had happened. They ran to the tomb and found it empty as Mary said (Luke 24:12, John 20:2-10).

In the meantime, the other women entered the tomb. They encountered two angels who gave them a message for the disciples (Matthew 28:5-8, Mark 16:5-8, Luke 24:3-8).

> 1) When Mary Magdalene came to the tomb the second time, Jesus appeared to her (Mark 16:9, John 20:11-17).

> 2) Jesus, then, showed Himself to the other women who were still on their way to give the angels' message to the disciples (Matthew 28:9-10).

> 3) Jesus next appeared to Peter (Luke 24:34, 1 Corinthians 15:5).

4) Later that afternoon, Jesus showed Himself to two disciples who were traveling to Emmaus (Mark 16:12-13, Luke 24:13-35).

5) That same evening, Jesus appeared to the disciples in Jerusalem (Thomas was absent) (Luke 24:36-43, John 20:19-25).

6) A week later, the second Sunday after the crucifixion, Jesus appeared when all eleven of the remaining Apostles were present (Mark 16:14, John 20:26-29).

7) The scene shifts to Galilee. The disciples had gone there as Jesus told them. Jesus appeared to them by the Sea of Galilee (John 21:1-23).

8) Sometime while the disciples were in Galilee, Jesus appeared to them on a mountain and gave them the Great Commission (Matthew 28:16-20, Mark 16:15-18).

9) Upon Jesus' instructions, the disciples returned to Jerusalem. Jesus appeared to them on the Mount of Olives and, while they watched, ascended to heaven (Mark 16:19-20, Luke 24:44-53, Acts 1:3-11).

10) Sometime before His ascension, Jesus appeared to over 500 of His disciples (1 Corinthians 15:6).

11) Jesus also appeared to His brother, James (1 Corinthians 15:7).

All of these eyewitness accounts give credibility to the fact that Jesus really did rise from the dead. One really odd thing about many of the appearances is that people, at first, didn't recognize Jesus. Details like this, don't fit the profile of hallucination or wish fulfillment. We can be sure that the appearances were real.

II.   A Choice Of Occupation (John 21:1-19)

Acts 1:3 says that Jesus gave many convincing proofs that He was alive. The fact that Jesus had died and risen from the dead, no doubt shattered the preconceived ideas the Apostles had about Jesus and the Kingdom He had come to establish. Before, they thought in terms of a physical, political kingdom in which they would hold high office. Those dreams of glory died along with Jesus. I believe that the Apostles went through a period of reexamination and reassessment of their lives and priorities during the time right after the resurrection. Things were no longer as they thought and they didn't quite know what to do.

John records Peter saying, "I'm going out to fish" (John 21:3 NIV). I think this was far more than a statement that he was going to fill in some slack time while the disciples waited for something to happen. I think that Peter was expressing a decision to get back into his fishing business. If so, it was a decision which several of the other Apostles shared. They agreed to join Peter.

John seems to put a lot of emphasis on the fact that the disciples didn't catch anything on their own. It was only after Jesus told them what to do that they brought in a catch. The lesson is that we don't get anywhere when we try to do things our way and in our own strength. It is Jesus who provides.

When Jesus finished giving the disciples breakfast, He confronted Peter with a choice. "…do you truly love me more than these?" (John 21:15 NIV) I think that Jesus was referring to the boats and the nets when He asked the question. In other words, "Peter, you've got to figure out what's important. I called you to fish for men. You have to decide whether you love me more than the fishing business. If you really love me you'll switch careers from being a fisherman to being a shepherd."

Fortunately, Peter and the other Apostles got their priorities right. They ditched the fishing business. From that point on, they gave their full time to spreading the Gospel.

III.   The Commission

It was shortly after the incident on the shore of the Sea of Galilee that Jesus gave the Apostles their life-work. Matthew records it this way, "Then the eleven disciples went to Galilee, to the mountain where Jesus had told them to go. When they saw him, they worshiped him; but some doubted. [Note: It's interesting that even after they saw "many convincing proofs" that Jesus was alive (Acts 1:3) some of the disciples still doubted!] Then Jesus came to them and said, "All authority in heaven and on earth has been given to me. Therefore go and make disciples of all nations, baptizing them in the name of the Father and of the Son and of the Holy Spirit, and teaching them to obey everything I have commanded you. And surely I am with you always, to the very end of the age.'"" (Matthew 28:16-20 NIV)

We call this "The Great Commission." It is worth noting that it is still in force. If we are to obey everything Jesus commanded the Apostles, it includes what He told them to do on this occasion. The command will remain in force until the "end of the age."

There are two parts to the commission. What are they?

> 1) Go and make disciples.

> 2) Teach them to obey everything.

Both parts are essential. You can't teach someone to obey without them first becoming a disciple. It's pointless to make disciples if it doesn't lead to change and growth.

In addition to the commission itself, Jesus gave the Apostles some specific instructions about how they were to carry it out. He told them to remain in Jerusalem until Holy Spirit empowered them (Acts 1:4-5). He went on to tell them about their ministry, "But you will receive power when the Holy Spirit comes on you; and you will be my witnesses in Jerusalem, and in all Judea and Samaria, and to the ends of the earth." (Acts 1:8 NIV).

The Greek word translated 'witness' in this passage is the same word from which we get our word 'martyr.' Jesus was telling the Apostles that they would have to give their lives in order to proclaim the Gospel. It says a lot about them that once they were convinced of the truth of the resurrection that they were willing to give their lives in order to preach it.

IV.   Farewell (Mark 16:19-20, Luke 24:44-53, Acts 1:3-11)

After commissioning the Apostles, Jesus left them by ascending into heaven. However, He also left with the promise that He would return. As Christians we live in that hope. One day Jesus will return and take us to be with Him forever.

What are the practical consequences of this hope?

> Peter writes, "But in keeping with his promise we are looking forward to a new heaven and a new earth, the home of righteousness. So then, dear friends, since you are looking forward to this, make every effort to be found spotless, blameless and at peace with him." (2 Peter 3:13-14 NIV) If the new heaven and earth is going to be the home of righteousness, it follows that everyone who lives there will also be righteous. Therefore, if we hope to live there, we need to be righteous. What does that say about the kind of lifestyle we're living? What about our thoughts and attitudes?

V.   Replacement (Acts 1:15-26)

Jesus instructed the Apostles to stay in Jerusalem until the coming of the Spirit. While they were waiting, they chose Matthias to take the place of Judas. With his choosing, the stage was set for the birth of the church.

VI.   Priorities

What about us? Do we believe in the resurrection? If we do, how does the resurrection affect our priorities?

What are we doing to fulfill the Great Commission? Are we making disciples? Are we teaching people to obey everything the Lord has commanded?

Do we live in the hope of Christ's return?

₧₨

Witnesses in Jerusalem

Introduction: The 50 days following Jesus' crucifixion was a time of profound re-examination and change for the disciples. Their understanding of who Jesus was and His mission underwent a profound change. They had to discard their preconceived notions of the Kingdom of Heaven. Once their ideas of the Kingdom were shattered, they had to make a choice whether they were going to return to their old occupations. To their credit, once they became convinced that Jesus had risen from the dead, they chose to become witnesses of the risen Lord. They left their old way of life behind.

Jesus instructed the Apostles to remain in Jerusalem until the Holy Spirit empowered them. After Jesus' ascension to heaven, they had to wait another 10 days, until Pentecost, before this happened.

What is Pentecost, and what does it mean?

> The word 'Pentecost' literally means 'fiftieth.' It refers to the fiftieth day after Passover, which always falls on Sunday. In the Old Testament, Pentecost is known as the Feast of Weeks. It was a harvest festival, celebrating the end of the grain harvest (Leviticus 23:15-22). It was the 2nd of the 3 "pilgrimage festivals" when all Jewish men were supposed to travel to Jerusalem.

> There was something else associated with Pentecost as well. It became a celebration of the giving of the Mosaic Law at Mt. Sinai. The Law of Moses was given 50 days after the first Passover. Just as the Old Covenant came into effect 50 days after Passover, the New Covenant was going to come into effect 50 days after the Lamb which takes away the sins of the world (the true Passover lamb) was sacrificed. This is just one of the many things the Old Covenant foreshadowed.

I. Power From On High (Acts 2:1-41)

In obedience to Jesus' command, the Apostles stayed in Jerusalem. With them were over 100 other disciples. While they were together on the morning of Pentecost, the Holy Spirit came upon them. There was a sound like a mighty wind, something which looked like tongues of fire came to rest on them and they were given the ability to speak in other languages.

> **Tangent:** There is some controversy over whether the Spirit empowered just the 12 Apostles or the whole group of 120. The Church of Christ has traditionally taught that the supernatural gifts were given only to the 12. However, there is no direct statement that this is so. A natural reading of the passage, particularly in light of the manifestation of the Spirit at the house of Cornelius which Acts 10 records, indicates that the Spirit came upon all 120 of the disciples. Whether the supernatural signs were given to the few or the many, what is certain is that it was the Apostles who preached to the crowds (Acts 2:14).

Upon hearing the sound, a large crowd gathered. Peter and the 11 other Apostles explained the phenomena as a fulfillment of prophecy. These signs pointed to the availability of salvation for everyone who would call on the name of the Lord.

Peter, then, preached to the crowd about Jesus. The outline of his sermon is something like this:

> 1) It's not what you think! This is from the Spirit.
>
> 2) God accredited Jesus by the miracles and works He performed among you.
>
> 3) You killed Him, but this was all according to God's plan.
>
> 4) God raised Jesus from the dead.
>
> 5) Jesus is exalted to the right hand of God.
>
> 6) This Jesus, whom you crucified, is both Lord and Christ. To put it another way, Jesus is the legitimate heir of David and also the Messiah for whom the nation of Israel had been waiting.

The effect of Peter's sermon was immediate and powerful. The crowd:

1) Believed. If the people had not believed what Peter told them, they would not have responded as they did.

2) Was convicted. The people not only realized that what Peter said was true, but what they had done was wrong.

3) Asked what they should do.

4) Immediately obeyed what they were told to do.

Lesson: We hear a lot about the necessity to believe or have faith. Faith and belief, however, are much more than acknowledging facts. True faith will always move a person to do. Unless faith prompts us to act, it is not faith. Actions prompted by faith are very different from so called 'works of merit'. In reality, such acts are faith in visible form.

What did Peter tell the crowd to do:

1) Repent. What is repentance?

> Literally, it means to change one's mind. We change the mindset which led us to commit sin to one which keeps us from sin. To express it another way, repentance is dying to self.

2) Be baptized for the forgiveness of sins. What is baptism all about?

> According to Romans 6, we are buried with Christ in baptism and raised to new life. We are clothed with Christ in baptism. It is the point at which we come under the blood of Christ, our sins are forgiven and we enter into a covenant relationship with God. Note that baptism is not a work of merit. It is an act of faith. It is not the act, or the water, per se, which saves, but God through the sacrifice of Jesus Christ.

3,000 people responded to Peter's message and were baptized that day.

Tangent: There have been skeptics who claim that there weren't pools big enough in Jerusalem to baptize so many people. That is totally false. There were several large pools in Jerusalem. Two of them were just outside the Temple complex. One of these was discovered just a few years ago during the construction of a pipeline next to the Temple Mount. It alone would have been more than big enough to handle the Pentecost crowd.

II.   The Church In The Beginning (Acts 2:42-47)

One of the intriguing questions about the church in Jerusalem is how it was organized. We aren't told how the Apostles managed to lead, teach and train such a large number of new converts. Something which must have helped a great deal is the core group of 120 disciples who had been with Jesus before the crucifixion. If these 120 each took a group of the new converts under their wings, the task would have become manageable. If the 3,000 were divided into house churches, only 60 groups of 50 each would have been needed. Also, many of the new converts would have been high-quality in the sense that they already knew the Scriptures and about the ministry of Christ. They could have been given leadership roles quite soon after their conversion.

While we do not know how the church was organized, we do know what the emphasis was. They devoted themselves to 4 things:

> 1) The Apostles' Teaching. The New Testament Scriptures had not yet been written. No doubt the Apostles not only interpreted the Old Testament and showed how the prophecies are fulfilled in Christ, but also gave their personal testimonies about what they had seen and heard as they ministered with Jesus. These eye-witness accounts were the equivalent of what we have in the four Gospels.

> 2) Fellowship. This implies that the people got to know each other. They formed a new community. They became a family. They ate together in their homes. Another unique characteristic of the church is that the people "had everything in common." This is often described as an early form of

Communism. However, there are several important differences.

a) No coercion was involved. The sharing of goods was strictly voluntary.

b) The concept of private property was still recognized and respected.

c) The purpose was not to redistribute wealth, but to meet needs.

3) The Breaking of Bread. This refers to Communion or the Lord's Supper. Contrary to the practice of many churches today, Communion was something the early church kept regularly. History tells us that they celebrated it each Lord's Day (Sunday).

4) Prayer. The early church was a praying church. The people were in regular communication with God.

These four areas should define the practice of the church today. Unfortunately, our congregations often fall short in one or more of them.

Another interesting thing about the early church is its perspective on growth. They recognized that it was not they, but God, who added to their number. This is something which the church growth experts would do well to remember. It is not what we do, but what God does, which causes the church to grow.

III.   A Gift More Precious Than Gold (Acts 3:1-4:31)

As Peter and John were going up to the Temple one day, a lame beggar asked them for money. Instead of giving money, Peter healed the man. Peter used this occasion to preach to the crowd which gathered – declaring that Jesus was the Christ and that He had risen from the dead. Many were converted because of what they heard. The number of men converts grew to about 5,000.

However, the Sadducees became upset, because Peter's message about the resurrection contradicted their belief system. They hauled

Peter and John before the Sanhedrin. When asked by what power or name they had healed the cripple, Peter proclaimed Christ to them. In the process, Peter laid the responsibility for Jesus' death at their door, just as he had earlier convicted the crowd of their complicity in it.

In contrast to the crowd, the response of the Sanhedrin was one of unbelief. They recognized that a miracle had been done, yet they would not turn to Christ through whom the miracle had been done. Instead, they tried to suppress the message.

Instead of being cowed by the threats of the authorities, Peter and John boldly told them that they would obey God and keep on speaking. They prayed for additional boldness to speak. God answered their prayer and they continued to proclaim Christ.

IV.   No Needy Among Them (Acts 4:32-5:11)

In addition to the external threats from the authorities, the young church also faced an internal threat. As already noted, people sold private possessions in order to meet the needs of others in the church. One man who sold a field and gave the money to the Apostles for distribution to the needy, was Barnabas.

Ananias and his wife Sapphira apparently wanted the reputation of being generous, without paying the cost. They sold a piece of property and gave some of the proceeds to the church. That was fine except they lied about it. They apparently took credit for giving the entire amount while keeping part. Both husband and wife died after being confronted with the truth. This dramatic consequence of hypocrisy had a very beneficial effect on everyone, both inside and outside the church. The result was fear. No doubt this kept many others from the temptation to try to feather their own nest by means of the church.

V.   Counted Worthy To Suffer (Acts 5:12-42)

The success of the church soon got the Apostles into trouble with the authorities again. The Sadducees had them arrested and put on trial before the Sanhedrin. On the advice of a Pharisee named Gamaliel, the court let the Apostles off with only a flogging and orders not to speak in Jesus' name.

Instead of being discouraged, the Apostles rejoiced that they were counted worthy to suffer for Jesus. They disobeyed the orders of the authorities and kept on talking about Jesus.

VI.   Forms Of Ministry (Acts 6:1-7)

With the church as large as it had become, there were bound to be some problems. Predictably, one of the serious ones had to do with interpersonal relationships. Even though the disciples had the attitude that their possessions were not their own, and shared everything they had, some needs fell through the cracks. One segment of the church felt that they were being neglected. Unfortunately, there was truth in the charge. Some of the needy had been overlooked.

> **Lesson:** Even the best attitude and the best will in the world is not enough. We need to go out of our way to find out how others are doing and what their needs are.

If we're not careful, the pressures of administration can interfere with what is more important. The Apostles realized that they could not handle everything themselves and needed to delegate. They would keep their emphasis on speaking, teaching and prayer, while turning the physical aspects of the church over to others. The Apostles set the criteria and let the church choose men who met the criteria. Then the Apostles formally appointed the men to the role. It is probable that the seven men who were chosen were the first deacons.

This division of responsibility is still important. The spiritual and physical needs of a congregation are too great for one set of men to handle. The needs in one area distract from the other. Elders need to be freed from the physical aspects of church administration so they can concentrate on the spiritual.

VII.   The First Martyr (Acts 6:8-8:1a)

Stephen, one of the seven who had been chosen, soon expanded his ministry from providing food to the Grecian widows to speaking in the Grecian synagogues. These so-called Grecian synagogues were composed of people who were ethnic, but expatriate, Jews who had migrated to Palestine. When these Jews could not refute Stephen's arguments, they resorted to false accusations of blasphemy.

The Jewish leaders seized Stephen and brought him before the Sanhedrin. Stephen preached a powerful sermon in which he pointed out that the authorities' rejection of Jesus was a continuation of Israel's resisting the Holy Spirit and rejection of God's prophets throughout history.

When Stephen concluded his address by proclaiming that he saw the Son of Man standing at the right hand of God, they dragged him out of the city and stoned him to death. As he was dying, Stephen forgave his murderers. One of the people who was there, approving of the murder, was Saul. Little did he know that, one day, he would boldly proclaim the very faith that Stephen died for.

VIII.   Something To Die For?

In this study we've mentioned several deaths.

> 1) There's the death to self which is necessary in order to enter into covenant relationship with God.

> 2) There was the death of the hypocrites, Ananias and Sapphira.

> 3) There was the death of the first martyr, Stephen.

We all need to evaluate ourselves. Have we died to self? If the Holy Spirit confronted us as He did Ananias and Sapphira, would we live or die? If someone were to put us on trial for our faith, would there be enough evidence to convict?

₧₧

Witnesses in Judea and Samaria

Introduction: The martyrdom of Stephen had far-reaching consequences. Though up to this point the church had enjoyed the favor of the people (Acts 5:13), and the authorities had done nothing more than threaten and flog the Apostles, a severe persecution broke out immediately after Stephen's death. It was as if having once tasted blood, the crowd's appetite for blood grew. The persecution was so severe that everyone except the Apostles scattered (Acts 8:1).

Why the persecution? Some suggest that the Apostles had been slow in fulfilling Christ's mandate to take the Gospel beyond Jerusalem. Therefore, God precipitated the persecution to get them moving. While this is possible, it seems unlikely. a) Though the Apostles remained in Jerusalem, their influence was not restricted to that city. The Gospel had already been preached, on the day of Pentecost, to many who were from regions outside of Jerusalem. The witness was going out even though the record emphasizes the church in Jerusalem. For example, it seems that the church in Rome came into existence without the direct involvement of the Apostles. b) Though the chronology is not certain, the persecution may have taken place as little as two or three years after the beginning of the church. The Apostles can hardly be accused of negligence for not personally evangelizing all of Judea and Samaria in that short a time. c) If the intent was to get the Apostles out of Jerusalem, the persecution was ineffective. The record specifically says that everyone but the Apostles scattered.

It's more likely that the persecution had nothing to do the Apostles' supposed slowness in fulfilling the Great Commission. Rather, God turned the evil schemes of men to His own advantage. The persecution merely hurried along something which would have happened anyway. Those who were scattered became evangelists.

Another consequence of the persecution was that it laid the groundwork for one of the most effective missionaries of all time. There is little doubt that one of the things which later drove Paul to proclaim the Gospel as he did was his sense of responsibility for the mayhem he had caused during this time (for example, see Philippians 3:4-14, 1 Timothy 1:12-13).

I.   Philip's Ministry (Acts 8:4-40)

One of the people who were scattered by the persecution was Philip. He was one of the seven the church chose to oversee food distribution to the widows. He went to a city in Samaria and began to preach and perform miracles. Many accepted the message and were baptized into Christ.

When the Apostles in Jerusalem heard about it, they sent Peter and John. Peter and John built on Philip's work. They placed their hands on the converts to give them the gift of the Holy Spirit.

Simon, who had been a sorcerer before his conversion tried to buy the ability to give the Holy Spirit. Peter rebuked him for his wickedness. It is from this incident that we get our word 'simony' which refers to buying or selling an ecclesiastical office or position. After dealing with Simon, Peter and John made their way back to Jerusalem, preaching in many Samaritan villages on the way.

> **Tangent:** There is a lot of controversy over the supernatural gifts of the Holy Spirit – whether they still exist and how they are/were given. From the record we have in the New Testament, it appears that, aside from the two incidents of Pentecost and at the house of Cornelius, people obtained the gifts only through the hands of the Apostles. For example, even though Philip had the ability to perform miracles, he could not pass it on. The Samaritans did not receive the gifts until after Peter and John arrived on the scene to place their hands on the converts. If this was the norm, and it appears that it was, then the gifts must have ceased shortly after the apostolic period. History seems to bear this out.

Philip began to preach somewhere north of Jerusalem, but the Spirit soon sent him southwest to the Jerusalem-Gaza road. There, he met an official from Ethiopia who was returning home after a pilgrimage to Jerusalem. Philip explained the Gospel to the official and baptized him into Christ. Unfortunately, Scripture does not tell us the sequel.

We do not know what happened when this man returned to court. Was he able to share his new faith with others? If a church came into existence in Ethiopia through this man's efforts, how did it receive further instruction and grounding in the faith? We do know from history that there was a very strong Christian presence in the area for several centuries. But we do not know the details.

> **Tangent:** We know little about the eunuch as a person. We do not know whether he was an ethnic Jew, or a convert to Judaism at the time of his pilgrimage. One thing we can say is that the stigma of ethnic origin or physical mutilation is removed in Christ. According to the Mosaic Law, no one who had a physical defect could serve as a priest offering sacrifices. He could not approach the altar or the curtain which separated the Holy Place in the Temple from the Holy of Holies. To do so desecrated the Sanctuary (Leviticus 21:17-23). In the New Covenant, what is important is not our background, but our submission to God's will (Isaiah 56:3-7, Galatians 3:28, Colossians 3:11).

After his encounter with the Ethiopian, Philip made his way over to the seacoast and, then, back up north to Caesarea. There, he apparently settled down and raised a family (Acts 21:8-9).

II.   Saul's Conversion And Early Ministry (Acts 9:1-31, 22:3-21, 26:1-20, Galatians 1:11-19)

In the meantime, Saul continued to persecute the church. He was not content to merely make things difficult for those who called attention to themselves in Jerusalem. By his own admission, Saul actively searched out and arrested many, even in other towns. We don't know how much blood he had on his hands, but he must have been responsible for the death of a large number of the disciples.

While Saul was on one of his trips, this time to Damascus in Syria, to arrest disciples and bring them to Jerusalem for trial, Jesus appeared to him and confronted him with the truth. It's a difficult thing to admit that you've based your life on a lie. It's to Saul's credit that he did not reject the truth, but changed. The incredible fanaticism he displayed in trying to destroy the faith, he now used to proclaim the Gospel.

> **Tangent:** Ananias was understandably concerned when the Lord told him to go minister to Saul. It took some convincing for Ananias to accept that the man who was perhaps the greatest enemy of the faith was ready to accept Christ. Would we have the faith to obey and proclaim Christ to someone like Saul? Could we see the potential in an enemy such as a member of the Taliban? Would we have the faith to welcome a former persecutor into our assemblies as the disciples in Damascus did?

Saul preached for a while in Damascus, proving that Jesus is the Christ. He then went into Arabia – probably to the area just east and south of Damascus, rather than the area we know as Arabia today. What he did there is obscure. Christ had told him that he was being sent to the Gentiles, but there is no record of his preaching in Arabia or of his winning any converts there. Some think that the time in Arabia after his conversion was spent in receiving special instruction by revelation from Christ.

About three years after his conversion Saul returned to Damascus from Arabia. He soon had to flee from there and he returned to Jerusalem. The church in Jerusalem had reconstituted itself after Saul's persecution ended, but the disciples were understandably wary of accepting their former persecutor. It wasn't until Barnabas brought him to the Apostles that the church accepted Saul as one of their own. When the church learned of a plot against Saul, the disciples sent him off to his home town of Tarsus, located in what is now the country of Turkey.

III.   Peter In Lydda And Joppa (Acts 9:32-43)

The scene now shifts back to Peter. While Saul was in Damascus and Arabia, Peter evangelized in the seacoast towns, west and north of Jerusalem. Because of the miracles he performed, many came to believe on the Lord.

IV.   Salvation Granted To The Gentiles (Acts 10:1-11:18)

Though Peter, himself, had preached on the day of Pentecost that the Lord would call those who were "far off" (Acts 2:39), he didn't seem to realize what that meant. It took a special manifestation of the Holy Spirit for him and the other Jewish believers to recognize and accept that Christ came to save Gentiles as well as Jews.

An angel told a devout Roman by the name of Cornelius to send for Peter. He did so and gathered a large group to hear whatever message Peter might have for them. While the messengers were on their way, Peter had a vision which prepared him to accept the summons.

Upon arriving at Cornelius' house, Peter preached to them about Christ. While he was speaking, the Holy Spirit came upon the group which was listening. Peter and the disciples with him took this as proof that God had accepted the Gentiles and ordered that they be baptized in the name of Christ. He then stayed a few days with the Gentile converts.

The fact that Peter had fraternized with and had preached to Gentiles opened him up to criticism from the other Apostles and Jewish believers. It was only when they heard that the Holy Spirit had been given to the Gentiles, just like He had to the Jewish believers at the beginning, that they realized that God was granting salvation to Gentiles, as well as Jews.

Tangent: The ministry of the Holy Spirit. There is a lot of confusion about how the Holy Spirit works in the lives of believers. The New Testament records three, distinct ways in which the Spirit impacted the early church.

> 1) The "baptism of the Spirit" (Mark 1:8, Acts 1:5, 11:16). The power of the Spirit suddenly fell upon the believers in a very visible and unmistakable way. The effects of this manifestation of the Spirit, such as speaking in tongues, were apparently beyond the control of the people affected. As far as we know from the scriptural record, the baptism of the Spirit occurred only twice – on the first Pentecost after Christ's resurrection (Acts 2:1-8), and at the house of

Cornelius (Acts 10:44-47). The purpose of the baptism was a) to authenticate that the Gospel message was from God, and b) to verify that God accepts non-Jewish people into the New Covenant.

2) The supernatural gifts of the Spirit (1 Corinthians 12:4-11). These gifts were temporary (1 Corinthians 13:8). They were needed to meet the needs of the church in the absence of the New Testament Scriptures. As far as we know, they were given only by the Apostles laying their hands on someone (for example, see Acts 8:18, Romans 1:11, 2 Timothy 1:6).

3) The indwelling of the Spirit (John 14:17, Romans 8:9, 11, 1 Corinthians 3:16, Ephesians 2:22, James 4:5). God lives in every Christian through His Spirit. The Spirit plays a vital role in the life of every Christian. For example, it is the Spirit who enables us to live godly lives (Galatians 5:16). He assures us of our salvation (Ephesians 1:14). He acts as a translator for us when we pray to God (Romans 8:26).

V.   Changes

In this chapter we've looked at several people who were confronted with change. The conversion of the Ethiopian eunuch challenged the Jewish attitude toward those who had physical handicaps. Saul had to change his whole idea about Jesus. The church had to change how it looked at Saul. The Jewish disciples had to change their ideas about Gentiles. What about us? In what ways do we need to change our ideas about who is acceptable to God? What wrong ideas or prejudices do we need to confront?

෪෬

Prelude to Expansion

Introduction: The conversion of Cornelius and the other Gentiles at his house was a major turning point in the history of the church. On the one hand, it opened up the preaching of the Gospel to the whole world. The promises God made in Eden and to Abraham were finally being fulfilled. All people, not just the Jews, were eligible to receive salvation.

On the other hand, the conversion of the Gentiles forced the Jewish believers to change their attitude toward people of other races. It also posed some difficult dilemmas. One was whether Gentiles had to keep the Mosaic Law. Eventually the church would have to confront and deal with this issue.

There were two more immediate problems. The first was not specific to Gentile conversions but had to do with growth: How could the church oversee and adequately train the new converts?

The second problem was related specifically to bringing Gentile people into fellowship. It had to do with the identity and culture of the church and affected the church's relationship to the broader Jewish community. Before, when all the followers of Christ were Jewish, the church could be considered just one more branch of the Jewish community. But with the inclusion of the Gentiles, that was no longer true. The church started to become something other than, and alien to, the Jewish community. This was to cause a lot of tension both within the church and for the church in its place in society.

I.   The Gospel Reaches Antioch (Acts 11:19-26)

To set the stage for what happened, we need to backtrack several years. The persecution which broke out after Stephen's martyrdom scattered the church in Jerusalem. Some of those who left, men who had originally come from Cyprus, traveled up the seacoast until they reached Antioch of Syria, located at the northeast corner of the Mediterranean Sea.

Far from being cowed by the persecution they had suffered, these men continued to preach the Gospel. At first they only spoke to Jews. Later, however – presumably after they heard about the conversion of Cornelius – they began to speak to Gentiles as well. God blessed their efforts and many were converted.

The news reached the church in Jerusalem and their response was the same as when they heard about the conversions in Samaria – they sent someone to help. They chose Barnabas. He was a logical choice. a) He was well respected and had the confidence of the Jerusalem church. b) He was full of the Holy Spirit (Acts 11:24). c) He also was from Cyprus (Acts 4:36), so would have had credibility with the men who were doing the work in Antioch.

Barnabas recognized that the work had God's blessing on it. As a result of his encouragement, many more were converted.

That, in itself, was a worthwhile outcome. But Barnabas did something else which had a tremendous impact on the future of the church. He traveled to Tarsus and hunted up Saul. Then he brought Saul back to Antioch to help teach. Prior to this time, Saul's ministry does not appear to have been very fruitful. At least there is no record of any success. That changed after he came to Antioch. From then on Saul became, arguably, the most successful missionary the church has ever known. This might not have happened if it hadn't been for Barnabas. It was Barnabas who recognized that Saul's conversion was genuine. It was Barnabas who vouched for Saul to the Apostles at Jerusalem. It was Barnabas who recognized Saul's potential and gave him the opportunity to become involved in the teaching ministry at Antioch. It was probably Barnabas who mentored and trained Saul to become what he did.

Question: Do we see the potential in other people? Are we able to look beyond their past to see what they can become?

II.   A New Name (Acts 11:26)

It was at Antioch that the followers of Christ got a new name. It was the name "Christian."

The name has become so common, and we are so used to it, that we don't give much thought to what it meant at the time. 'Christian' is a strange word, in that it is formed from a Greek title (Christ) with a Latin suffix (ian).

What does the suffix 'ian' mean?

> The suffix 'ian' has several meanings:
>
> 1) Belonging to – for example, a 'plebeian' is someone who belongs to the class of 'common people'.
>
> 2) Coming from – for example, a 'Canadian' is someone who comes from, or is a citizen of Canada.
>
> 3) Being involved in or with – for example, an 'electrician' is someone who deals with electricity (specifically someone who installs and maintains electrical wiring and equipment).
>
> 4) Resembles – for example, if someone is 'reptilian' he looks or behaves like a reptile.
>
> Therefore, the word 'Christian' refers to someone who belongs to, is involved with or resembles Christ. Christ is his occupation and identity.

It's worth noting that it was those outside the faith who applied the name to the disciples, and it probably was not meant as a compliment. The word is used in only two other places in the New Testament. One mention is in King Agrippa's remark to Paul, "Do you think that in such a short time you can persuade me to be a Christian?" (Acts 26:28 NIV) We do not know in what tone of voice the king said this, but it is quite possible he said it with contempt.

The other place is in 1st Peter 4:16 where Peter tells the disciples not to be ashamed of the name. Peter was writing about persecution. From the point of view of a persecutor, to be a Christian is as dishonorable as being a thief or murderer. In this context, it's interesting that the followers of Christ did not use the name 'Christian' for themselves, for about the first 100 years.

However, there is another side to this. The prophet Isaiah prophesied that God would give His people a new name. (See Isaiah 62:2.) There are many names used for Jesus' followers, such as disciples (Acts 6:7), saints (Ephesians 1:1), brothers (Acts 15:1, 23) and followers of the Way (Acts 9:2). The only name, however, that can be applied exclusively to Jesus' followers is 'Christian.'

Question: If we didn't call ourselves Christians, could people tell that we belonged to Christ anyway? Do our words, our actions, and our character show that we are His disciples? Are we ashamed of the label?

III.   Famine Relief (Acts 11:27-30, 12:25)

The church at Antioch was unique in that, as far as we know, it was the first church in which both Jews and Gentiles worshiped and fellowshipped together in unity. They soon got an opportunity to demonstrate unity in a wider sense.

The church in Jerusalem had already shown their approval and acceptance of the Antioch church be sending Barnabas to them. The people in the church at Antioch got the opportunity to reciprocate when they learned that a famine was coming. They decided to help the brothers in Judea through the hard times by sending a gift. They chose Barnabas and Saul to take this gift.

IV.   Apostles In Danger (Acts 12:1-24)

The chronology is a little hard to reconstruct so we don't know exactly how the mission to provide famine relief is connected to the incidents which Luke records in Acts 12. Many commentators think that Paul refers to the famine mission in Galatians 2:1. If so, it took place about three years after Herod's death (AD 44), and Acts 12 is out of chronological order.

Assuming, however, that Galatians 2:1 refers to the Jerusalem Council which Acts 15 records, it's possible that Barnabas and Saul arrived in the middle of the persecution Herod directed at the Apostles. It's even possible that the famine relief mission served as one of the triggers for Herod's persecution. This is entirely speculative, without any direct support in Scripture, but could the prejudice against the leaders of the Jerusalem church have been caused by their willingness to accept help from Gentile sources and, even worse, accept Gentiles as God's people?

> **Application:** When we help others, we need to think about the possible consequences. We need to not only help, but help in such a way that it won't cause problems for the recipients. Years later, when Paul brought another offering to the Jerusalem church, they told him that it would cause a severe public-relations problem. Paul then complied with the solution the church asked him to implement in order to diffuse the situation. It backfired, in that Paul was arrested, but it got the church off the hook.

In any case, Luke records that Herod (this is the grandson of the Herod who killed the babies in Bethlehem) executed James, the brother of John. Though the church had originally enjoyed the favor of the people (Acts 2:47, 5:13), now James' execution pleased the Jews (Acts 12:3).

Peter was next on the list. However, on the eve of his trial, an angel miraculously rescued Peter from prison. Even though the Christians in Jerusalem were praying for Peter, they were still astonished when their prayers were answered. It took Peter some time to convince them that he really was alive and free.

After telling the brothers what had happened, Peter went into hiding. It's significant that he specifically told them to inform James. This signals an important change in the leadership of the church. Change had already started to occur, for Acts 11:30 mentions Elders. Though the Apostles still had an important role, they had begun to relinquish control of the local congregations. This incident hastened the process. From this point on, it is not Peter, but James "the Just", who is the most prominent of the leaders in the Jerusalem church.

The selection of James might have been important from another standpoint. James was well known for his piety and for scrupulously keeping the Law. His taking a prominent role in the church may have helped quiet the opposition raised by the church's having accepted Gentile believers.

V.   The Book Of James

The situation in Antioch and other places, plus James' death and Peter's narrow escape, highlighted the tremendous challenges the Apostles faced.

> 1) The church had spread to places where it was physically impossible for the Apostles to personally oversee it. How could they fulfill the second part of the Great Commission – to teach the disciples everything Jesus had commanded (Matthew 28:20)?

> 2) James' death made it obvious that the Apostles were a 'wasting asset,' a temporary resource. The time would come when they would die. Both James and Peter were in Jesus' inner circle. Both were taken out of circulation by Herod's persecution. How could the Apostles preserve the teaching for future generations?

One answer to the dilemma was to write the teachings down. It was probably shortly after Herod's persecution that one of the Apostles penned the first of the New Testament books. It is the book of James. It's not entirely clear which James wrote the book, but it's likely that it was James, the son of Alphaeus, who was one of the 12.

The book was written to those who were scattered (1:1). It was written to give reassurance to those who were going through trials (1:12). The theme of the book is putting our faith into practice (1:22). In fact, James is one of the most down-to-earth, practical books in the entire New Testament. Yes, it does touch on doctrine, but the emphasis is on lifestyle. How should the disciples put their new-found faith into practice?

Luther dismissed James as "a book of straw." In his view it teaches justification by works instead of by faith. But Luther misunderstood the message. James does not dismiss faith or substitute works for faith. Instead, he points out that obedience is the natural outgrowth of faith. Faith without action is dead (2:17).

Luther also felt that James should be discounted because it does not mention the work of the Spirit. Again, Luther missed James' message. In fact, James writes about every one of the fruits of the Spirit mentioned in Galatians 5:22-23).

Love (2:8)

Joy (1:2)

Peace (3:17)

Patience (5:7)

Kindness (2:13)

Goodness (3:17)

Faithfulness (2:14)

Gentleness (3:13, 4:6)

Self control (1:26, 3:1-2)

When viewed in context, the book of James was precisely what the early believers needed to help them through the situations they faced. It is still just as relevant today.

Question: Will we listen to the teaching and apply it to our lives, or will we dismiss it as irrelevant like Luther did?

ೞೞ

Targeting the Gentiles

Introduction: The church began in Jerusalem and, for many years, Jerusalem was the center to which all the followers of Christ looked. Jerusalem was where the Apostles were. Jerusalem was the place from which the first missionary efforts originated. The early disciples were Jews and the center of Jewish culture and tradition was the Temple, which was located in Jerusalem.

After a dozen years or so, however, the focus shifted to Antioch. There were several factors in this shift.

> 1) Several waves of persecution in Jerusalem scattered many of the disciples. As a result, new congregations came into being in many other places. This diluted the influence of the Jerusalem church.

> 2) The Apostles turned the responsibility of leading the Jerusalem church over to others and went out on evangelistic tours. While the Apostles were absent from Jerusalem, their authority was absent also.

> 3) An extraordinarily talented and strong leadership developed in Antioch.

> 4) Antioch was better able to minister to non-Jewish converts than the church in Jerusalem. As people of Gentile origin began to make up a larger and larger proportion of the church, it was natural that Antioch would have greater influence with them than Jerusalem.

> 5) In comparison with Antioch, Jerusalem was a relatively poor church. Antioch provided aid to Jerusalem.

> 6) Most importantly, the Holy Spirit chose Antioch as the starting place for the next major evangelistic thrust.

I.   Set Apart For The Work (Acts 13:1-3)

Why is it that the Holy Spirit chooses one person for a particular purpose and not another? What makes one congregation more suitable than another to fulfill a divine mission? The answer is not always obvious. Sometimes God chooses people and congregations who, from a human point of view, appear ill-equipped or unsuited for the purpose. However, Barnabas, Saul and the church at Antioch had several characteristics which qualified them for the task God wanted done.

1) They were open to the Spirit's voice. It was while they were worshiping and fasting that the Spirit told them to set Barnabas and Saul apart. There's an important principle here. God is more likely to accomplish His will through those who are already trying to understand and do His will. As one of the Old Testament prophets said to King Asa, "…The LORD is with you when you are with him. If you seek him, he will be found by you, but if you forsake him, he will forsake you." (2 Chronicles 15:2 NIV)

2) Barnabas and Saul were willing to go. Yes, God can do great things through people who are reluctant, but it is easier all around when they are willing. For example, Barnabas and Saul make quite a contrast to Moses. They didn't argue with God and try to get out of the assignment like Moses did (Exodus 3:11-4:13). God got angry with Moses (Exodus 4:14). In contrast, Barnabas and Saul enjoyed the blessing of the Spirit (Acts 13:4).

3) The church was willing to send them. Good teachers are hard to come by. It's not everyone who has deep insights into the Word and is able to convey those insights in a meaningful way to others. It must have been hard for the church at Antioch to let Barnabas and Saul go. Part of the growth at Antioch resulted from their work. Yet, the church was willing to put the interests of others ahead of their own. More importantly, they were willing to obey the direction of the Spirit. They were wise enough to know that obedience was, in fact, their best interest.

Question: Are we as discerning? Do we base our decisions on selfishness, or on what is best for others? Are we obedient?

4) Barnabas and Saul could leave because they had trained others to take over their responsibilities so that the church was not crippled by their absence. Barnabas and Saul had trained the church at Antioch to be self-reliant in the sense that it was not dependent on the work of one or two gifted leaders. This, as we shall see, was an important principle which played a major role in the evangelistic tour that Barnabas and Saul made.

Historical Note: How big was the church at Antioch? During the apostolic period the total population of Antioch was about 500,000. Over time, this declined until around 400 AD the total free (non slave) population stood at about 200,000, half of which were Christians. During the apostolic period the church would have been much smaller. Still, it's not unreasonable to assume that it numbered up to several thousand at the time of the missionary journeys.

II.   Turning Point On Cyprus (Acts 13:4-12)

While the Spirit clearly told Barnabas and Saul to go, we have no indication that the Spirit told them where to go. In the absence of clear instructions to do otherwise, it was natural for the two men to go to Cyprus (Acts 13:4). This was the place from where Barnabas came (Acts 4:36) and would have been familiar territory to him.

When Barnabas and Saul returned to Antioch from their famine-relief mission to Jerusalem, they brought John-Mark, who was Barnabas' cousin (Colossians 4:10), with them (Acts 12:25). Mark came along on this journey too, as a helper (Acts 13:5). The text does not say so, but it is quite probable that Mark was another person whose potential Barnabas recognized, and whom he made a deliberate effort to mentor and train.

The trio traveled throughout Cyprus preaching the Gospel. The account indicates, however, that their initial efforts were confined to reaching the Jewish people and whatever "God-fearing" Gentiles there might be in the synagogues (Acts 13:5). This pattern changed when they reached the city of Paphos.

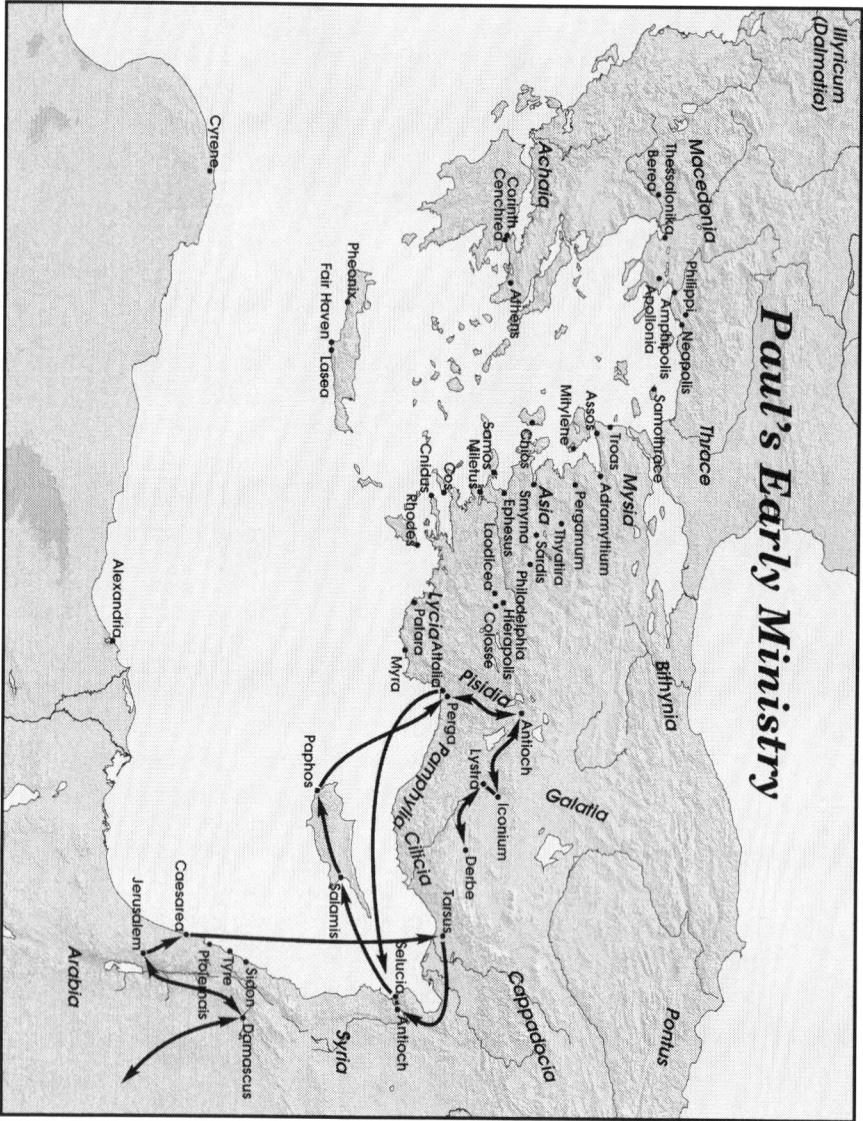

Paul's Early Ministry

At Paphos, the Roman proconsul ordered them to appear before him and explain the Gospel. (The word 'proconsul' means governor or military commander. This man was the highest Roman authority on Cyprus.) While the proconsul wanted to listen to God's word (Acts 13:7), his Jewish court magician tried to prevent him from believing (Act 13:8). This parallels the situation which occurred when Philip preached to the Samaritans and Simon the sorcerer tried to pervert the gifts of the Spirit (Acts 8:9-24).

Another parallel is with Saul's own conversion. Jesus struck Saul blind while confronting him. Here Saul, full of the Holy Spirit, struck Elymas blind while confronting him.

The immediate result of this confrontation was that the proconsul, Sergius Paulus, believed. But it also had two other important and far-reaching consequences.

> 1) As far as we know, this was the first time that Barnabas and Saul had spoken directly to a Gentile audience. Always before they had preached to Gentiles who were already attending the synagogues. The contrast between the proconsul and Elymas must have been an eye-opening experience. Here was a Gentile who was eager to hear the Gospel while a Jew, who was the natural recipient of the Word, opposed it. Apparently it was this incident which convinced Saul that the Gentiles could be approached directly. It's interesting to note, that from this point on, Scripture refers to him by his Gentile name of Paul. This change of name seems to reflect his change in emphasis.

> 2) Up to this point, the book of Acts always lists Barnabas' name first. This is an indication that Barnabas led the mission. Barnabas was the mentor and Saul the disciple. From this incident forward, Paul's name is sometimes listed first. This is an indication that Paul was starting to come into his own. The mentoring had paid off. Paul was learning to take the lead.

III.   We Had To Speak To You First (Acts 13:13-52)

From Cyprus, Paul and Barnabas traveled to the mainland. On their arrival, something else happened which had major implications for the future. John-Mark deserted them (Acts 15:38) and returned to Jerusalem (Acts 13:13).

The text does not say why John-Mark left. There are several theories. Some think that he was frightened or intimidated by the dangers of traveling inland. Others think that Paul's illness may have been more than he could stomach (see Galatians 4:13). But John-Mark's desertion may have had more to do with principle, or loyalty to Barnabas, than personal weakness. Was he upset that Paul was starting to take precedence over Barnabas? Did he resent the fact that Paul was starting to show leadership and determine where they went? More importantly, did John-Mark disapprove of the shift to preaching directly to the Gentiles? Did he feel that Paul had betrayed the cause? Some people speculate that John-Mark reported what Paul was doing to the Jerusalem church and this precipitated the crisis which led to the Jerusalem Council which Acts 15 records.

Whatever the cause of the rift, Paul and John-Mark eventually healed the estrangement between them. They were later able to work together again (Philemon 1:24). Paul also acknowledged that John-Mark was useful to him (2 Timothy 4:11).

For some reason Paul and Barnabas traveled inland to Pisidian Antioch. Paul later wrote that he had preached in the province of Galatia in inner Asia Minor because of an illness (Galatians 4:13). Was it because he needed to get away from the coast to the healthier highlands which prompted the choice of where to preach?

Whatever the reason, the synagogue rulers at Antioch invited Paul to preach. He addressed his message to both the Jews and the God-fearing Gentiles who were there. His sermon was similar to Stephen's sermon before the Sanhedrin (Acts 7:1-53). Did Paul model his sermon after what he heard Stephen say that day? If so, there was an important difference. While recounting Israel's history, Stephen emphasized the Jews' continuing pattern of disobedience. Paul, while going over the same history, pointed out that Jesus was the fulfillment of all Israel's hopes.

At first, the response was very positive. The Gentiles in particular were eager to hear more. But on the next Sabbath when almost the whole city came to hear God's word, the Jews became jealous and started opposing the message. This opposition confirmed the decision to turn to the Gentiles with the Gospel.

Question: What are our motives for opposing somebody or what they teach? Is it because they are not teaching the truth, or is it because of jealousy or some other wrong motive?

The experience at Pisidian Antioch set the pattern for the rest of Paul's ministry. On entering a new town, he would first approach the Jews with the Gospel. After they rejected it, he would turn his attention to preaching to the Gentiles.

Unfortunately, the Jews were often not content with rejecting the Gospel for themselves. They also tried to stop the message reaching anyone. They stirred up opposition and persecution against Paul and Barnabas and forced them to move on. In spite of the persecution, those who had been converted "were filled with joy and with the Holy Spirit." (Acts 13:52)

Question: What is our reaction to opposition or persecution? Can we rejoice in spite of trouble and suffering? Can others see the fruit of the Spirit in our lives?

After being forced to leave Antioch, Paul and Barnabas went to Iconium. They had great success there, but after some time were forced to move on again (Acts 14:1-7). They went on to preach in Lystra and Derbe and the surrounding countryside (Acts 14:6).

IV.   The Gods Have Come Down To Us! (Acts 14:1-20)

At Lystra a series of unpredictable events occurred which illustrate the hazards of missionary work. After Paul healed a man who had been lame from birth, the crowd proclaimed that he and Barnabas were gods. (It's interesting to note that they called Barnabas, Zeus which seems to indicate that they thought he was the leader, since Zeus was the chief god of the Greek pantheon. They called Paul, Hermes – the messenger of the gods, since he was the primary speaker.)

It was only with difficulty that Paul and Barnabas were able to get the crowd to refrain from sacrificing to them (Acts 14:18). Such is the fickleness of crowds, however, that just a short time later the people turned on Paul and stoned him. It seems miraculous that after being left for dead, Paul was able to get up and return to the city, and was fit enough the next day to move on to Derbe.

V.   Return Home (Acts 14:21-28)

From Derbe it seems that the logical thing to do would be to continue traveling east and then south, back to Syrian Antioch from where they had started. Instead, Barnabas and Paul decided to retrace their steps to Pisidian Antioch, visiting all the churches they had planted on the way. This took considerable courage as they had been persecuted in each town. They had not only been persecuted in Pisidian Antioch, but formally expelled (Acts 13:50).

There were two reasons for visiting the churches again. One was to encourage and strengthen the believers (Acts 14:22). The second reason, was to appoint Elders in every church (Acts 14:23). It was this important principle – teaching and enabling the disciples to govern themselves without relying on the talents and presence of the church planter which was one of the keys to the rapid and widespread growth of the church.

After arriving at the seacoast, Paul and Barnabas sailed back to Antioch of Syria. There they reported to the church what they had done. There is an important lesson in this – the principle of accountability. In spite of the fact that these men had been called by the Holy Spirit for the work they had done, they had been set aside, and commissioned by the church. Though sent by the Holy Spirit, they still reported back to the people who had ordained them for the work by laying their hands on them.

Lesson: Being called by God does not absolve us from accountability. It does not place us above authority.

෴

What to Do With the Gentiles?

Introduction: After the events at the house of Cornelius (Acts 10), there could be no doubt that God intended to include Gentile people in redemption. A restored relationship to God was no longer the exclusive domain of the Jews. Jesus came to save the whole world, not just the physical descendants of Abraham through Isaac (John 1:29).

As revolutionary as that thought was to the Jewish church, it implied an even more troubling corollary: If Gentiles were to be brought to faith in Christ, someone had to preach the Gospel to them. Since the first Christians were all Jews, it was obvious that the first evangelists to the Gentiles had to be Jews. To a certain extent, the Jews were already evangelistic in that they sought converts to Judaism (Matthew 23:15). But, paradoxically, associating with Gentiles risked the condemnation and censure of other Jews (Acts 11:1-3, Galatians 2:11-12). Therefore, it took courage for the first Christians to reach across the lines. We cannot know for certain, but from the evidence we have, it's reasonable to assume that most of the early outreach to Gentiles took place among the so-called "God-fearing Gentiles" – those who attended the synagogue and were attracted to the ethical teachings of Judaism, while not necessarily keeping the Mosaic Law.

This is certainly the pattern that Barnabas and Saul followed while they were on Cyprus during their first missionary journey (Acts 13:4-5). After their encounter with the proconsul, Sergius Paulus, however, Saul apparently realized that it was possible to approach Gentiles directly with the Gospel. He would no longer limit his evangelism to the "God-fearers". His switch to using his Roman name, Paul, seems to reflect the change in emphasis. Yes, upon entering a new town Paul would still speak to the Jews and "God-fearing" Gentiles first but, after being rejected at the synagogue, he would not move to a different synagogue – he turned directly to the Gentiles whether they had any connection to the synagogue or not. And so, the church reached another milestone in Gentile evangelism.

There were still some important questions the church had not thought through at the time of Cornelius' conversion. As more and more Gentiles were converted; as a larger percentage of the church became Gentile, it became essential to answer those questions. How was the church to regard these Gentiles who came to Christ? Were they now some kind of Jew? Was it necessary for someone to become a Jew in order to be a Christian? Were the Gentile converts required to keep the Mosaic Law?

To a large extent, these questions were really just a reflection of an even more fundamental question: What did Jesus mean when He said that He had come to fulfill the Law?

I.   A Breach Of The Peace (Acts 15:1-5)

Sometime it's best just to let sleeping dogs lie. In other words, not all questions or differences of opinion need to be aired. On the other hand, some questions need to be dealt with or they will destroy the church. Such was the case when some men came from Jerusalem to Antioch of Syria and started teaching that Gentile converts had to obey the Mosaic Law. They did not present it as an option, or even as something which was not required, but highly beneficial. They made it a matter of salvation.

Naturally, this would have thrown Gentile converts into confusion. Was the Gospel they heard incomplete? Even worse, was the Gospel they had been taught a false Gospel? Paul and Barnabas could not sit by and watch the faith of the Gentile converts undermined, so they engaged in a sharp dispute with these men.

The issues raised were so important, and had such wide implications, that the church in Antioch sent Paul and Barnabas with a whole delegation to Jerusalem to consult with the Apostles and Elders. On the way there, the delegation spread the news to other congregations about how the Gentiles had been converted (Acts 15:3). To the churches' credit, instead of feeling threatened by it, they welcomed the news. The church in Jerusalem also welcomed the delegation from Antioch. The Antioch delegation then made a presentation to the Apostles and Elders about what God had done through them.

In spite of the welcome, the issue of whether the Gentiles had to obey the law was contentious. Some of the Jewish believers were also Pharisees. The Pharisees were a group who had dedicated themselves to keeping the Law of Moses. Their name means 'The Separated Ones.' Many of them, even those who were not Christians, made an honest effort to rise above the level of the ordinary person and live truly holy and pure lives. In light of their background, it is no surprise that they insisted that everyone had to keep the Law in order to be saved. Paul, who himself had been a Pharisee (Philippians 3:5), did not agree. He saw a different principle at work.

II.   Resolution (Acts 15:6-21)

The Apostles and Elders met to give a definitive answer to this problem. Is faith in Christ sufficient to save, or do we need faith plus the Law?

There is controversy whether the meeting Paul describes in Galatians 2:1-10 refers to this Council, or to the famine relief mission which Acts 11:29-30 mentions. Assuming that Paul refers to the Jerusalem Council of Acts 15, we learn some interesting things about it from what Paul says.

> 1) The Apostles discussed and settled the issue privately before bringing it before the whole church (Galatians 2:2). Actually, saying that they settled it is a little misleading as they discovered that they were already in perfect agreement. There was no difference at all in the Gospel they all preached (Galatians 2:6-9).

> It says a lot about the Apostles and their leadership style that they allowed the congregation, particularly those who had contrary opinions, to speak and present their case even though the decision had already been made. They led by persuasion, not by imposing their own will. Though they had the authority to simply say, "This is the way it is", they gave opportunity for others to come to the right conclusion through discussion and examining the evidence for themselves.

Question: What is our style of leadership? Do we exercise authority and issue commands, or do we lead by example and persuasion?

2) Paul brought Titus along as a test case (Galatians 2:3). It says a lot about Titus that he was willing to go along with this. He was willing to do whatever was right. His love for Christ was stronger than personal pain. If the Apostles said it was necessary for him to be circumcised, he was willing to go along with it.

It also says a lot about the Apostles that they did not require Titus to be circumcised. They were willing to stand on principle rather than expediency. No doubt to have Titus circumcised would have saved them some temporary criticism from people in the Jerusalem church. But they took the long view and would not compromise the Gospel.

Question: How willing are we to do what is right even at the price of pain or inconvenience?

3) Paul calls the people who raised the issue "false brothers" (Galatians 2:4). At least some of those who took the position that Gentile converts had to keep the Law were not acting from principle, but from impure motives.

The Apostles let the discussion go on for a long time (Acts 15:7). Then, Peter reminded everyone how God had first given Gentiles the opportunity to hear the Gospel. God had not imposed the Law on them. On the contrary, He had accepted them in their uncircumcised state and had made no distinction between Jew and Gentile.

Paul and Barnabas gave further evidence of God's acceptance of the Gentiles by citing their own experiences. Finally, James showed how all this agreed with Scripture. Both God's Word and actual experience demonstrated that the Gentiles did not need Moses in addition to Christ.

III.   Apostolic Ruling (Acts 15:22-35)

The arguments won the support of the whole church (Acts 15:22) and they agreed to implement James' suggestion that they write a letter to the Gentile churches outlining the position they had come to. There are several noteworthy things about this letter:

> 1) It was not from the Apostles alone, but also from the Elders of the Jerusalem church. This raises an interesting question: Why did the Apostles involve the Jerusalem church? Why didn't the Apostles simply issue a ruling, particularly if, as Galatians seems to indicate, they had already decided the issue before bringing it to the church? As the "mother church" did Jerusalem have authority or jurisdiction over churches in other places?

>> The answer to this question is contained in the first part of the letter. People from the Jerusalem church caused the disturbance (Acts 15:24). Therefore, it was fitting for the church to be involved in correcting the situation. The deliberations of the Jerusalem Council did not just settle a thorny theological problem, they were also an act of local church discipline of unruly members who had started preaching a Gospel which was contrary to what the church sanctioned and taught. Far from exercising authority or claiming jurisdiction over anyone else, the church in Jerusalem apologized for some of their members who had overstepped their authority.

> **Question:** How willing are we to clean up the messes people in our congregation create? Do we just ignore our responsibility to other people and congregations?

> 2) In addition to sending the letter, the church also sent Judas and Silas to confirm the message (Acts 15:27). By doing this, no one could possibly accuse the delegation from Antioch of somehow twisting or misconstruing the Council's decision.

> Sending Judas and Silas also demonstrated the openness and transparency of the leaders of the Jerusalem church. They

didn't have anything to hide. If there were questions; if clarification was needed on some point, these men were there to provide the explanation.

Question: How transparent are we? Do we give people the opportunity to ask questions, or do we merely give directives?

3) The directives the Apostles and Elders gave were not their personal opinion. They were given through the Holy Spirit (Acts 15:28).

Question: How open to the leading of the Spirit are we, particularly when deciding how to address controversial issues? Do we actively try to determine the truth and God's will, or are we influenced by what is politically correct or expedient?

4) Many commentaries suggest that the prohibitions listed were included as a pragmatic way to ease the tensions between Jew and Gentile. While not required to keep the whole Law, the Gentiles should keep those portions of it about which the Jews were most sensitive. While the prohibitions certainly would have helped to ease discomfort between Jewish and Gentile believers, I think they were given for a much more fundamental reason. I think they are still in force even though Gentiles, for the most part, no longer have to worry about what Jews might think of them. In fact, to say Gentiles do not have to keep the Law except certain parts is contradictory and negates the very argument the Apostles and Elders made. No, Jesus fulfilled the whole Law, not just certain parts of it.

If the prohibitions are not based on the Mosaic Law, what are they based on? They are based on universal principles.

> a) Food sacrificed to idols. This speaks to our basic allegiance. If we belong to Christ, we cannot hold onto the old ways and lifestyle. We are to be a separate people belonging to God (1 Peter 2:9). Christianity is not syncretistic. We have to make a

choice whom we will worship – the idols, or God, through Christ. We cannot merely add Christ to our existing belief system. Paul later took up the issue of eating sacrificial meat with the Corinthians. He pointed out that eating meat sacrificed to idols is to commune with demons (1 Corinthians 10:20-22). We can't commune with demons and expect to have a relationship with Christ.

b) Blood. This prohibition refers back to the covenant God made with Noah (Genesis 9:1-17). There God said that life is in the blood, and forbade man to eat meat that still has blood in it (Genesis 9:4). Therefore, to eat blood, or meat with blood still in it (as in strangled animals) is to show contempt for a universal directive that God gave to the whole human race, long before the Mosaic Law.

By extension, the prohibition about blood reflects our basic view about the sanctity of life. God said that the reason He would demand an accounting from anyone who shed man's blood was that man is made in God's image (Genesis 9:5-6). Therefore, to kill a human being is to kill God in effigy.

c) Sexual immorality. This prohibition has to do with our most basic social relationships. The sexual act is not merely something physical. It also involves the spirit. When God instituted marriage in the Garden of Eden, He said that a man and woman would be 'united' and become 'one flesh' (Genesis 2:24). The literal idea is that they would become a single organism.

Paul explained the spiritual ramifications of this in 1 Corinthians 6:13-20. As believers in Christ, we are members of Christ's body. Our "...bodies are members of Christ himself' (1 Corinthians 6:15 NIV). Therefore to have sexual relations with a prostitute is to unite Christ's body with her. In contrast, we are to be united with Christ in spirit (1 Corinthians 6:17).

In short, the prohibitions have nothing to do with keeping the Mosaic Law or making Jewish Christians feel more comfortable. They have everything to do with basic principles of living for Christ.

The letter had the desired effect. The people "...were glad for its encouraging message." (Acts 15:31 NIV) The church had spoken decisively. From now on whoever tried to bind the Mosaic Law on Gentile converts could do so only by contradicting the Apostolic ruling.

IV.   The Letter To The Galatians

There is controversy over when Paul wrote the letter to the Galatians. Some date it before the Jerusalem Council. If so, it shows just how far the heresy had spread on which the Council ruled. The more likely possibility is that Paul wrote the letter from Corinth during his second missionary journey, or from Antioch of Syria after the journey. Whenever it was written, I include it here because it deals with the same theme as the Jerusalem Council.

Teachers showed up at the churches Paul planted in the province of Galatia proclaiming a different Gospel than Paul had. They claimed that faith in Christ is not enough. It is also necessary to keep the Mosaic Law in order to be saved. The churches were inclined to agree, but had the foresight to send a delegation to Paul with questions about this doctrine.

Paul's reply was that there is only one Gospel, and that to change it is to bring destruction and condemnation on oneself. He went on to contrast the two systems – of law and of faith. Law leads to slavery, while faith leads to liberty.

If law is not the answer for attaining holiness, what is? Paul's answer is that righteousness and holy conduct are a natural byproduct or result (fruit) of having God's Spirit indwell us. When we have the Spirit the Law does not apply. Under Law we try to do what is right through our own efforts and are doomed to failure. In the Spirit we are a new creation who does what is right, not through our own strength, but through His.

It's significant that Paul never mentions the ruling or letter from the Jerusalem Council, either in his letter to the Galatians, or anywhere else. Some speculate it is because Paul didn't agree with the ruling and it's prohibitions. That cannot be the case, because the record clearly states that Paul delivered the Council's decision to the churches he visited (Acts 16:4). Why, then, didn't Paul answer those who were upsetting the churches by simply referring to the decision the Apostles in Jerusalem had made?

> We don't know for sure, but here is one possibility: As humans we like system and rules. "Just tell me what to do and I'll do it!" Had Paul merely pointed to the letter the Council had written, it would have been easy for people to regard it as a replacement for the Law. The result would be to substitute one law for another. Paul was after something much more profound. He wanted people to experience life in the Spirit. He didn't want them to think in terms of rules and boundaries but of becoming like Christ.

Question: How do we live our lives? By rote, or by principle? Have we put our hope in a system, or in Christ? Do we do right things because we're trying to earn our way, or because they are the natural result of the Spirit in our hearts?

ഇറ

On to Europe

Introduction: The Jerusalem Council removed the last theological barrier to evangelizing Gentiles and welcoming them as full partners and brothers in Christ. They did not have to become Jews first, and Christians second. The decision also removed whatever racial or prejudicial hangups Gentiles might have had about coming to Christ. While all peoples become one in Christ (Colossians 3:11), becoming a Christian did not mean giving up one's own ethnic and cultural heritage. You could remain a Greek, Roman, Barbarian, Scythian or any other nationality and still be a Christian. This set the stage for worldwide evangelism. As Paul had already discovered, Gentiles could be approached directly with the Gospel.

From now on, the biggest impediment to evangelism would be human factors rather than theology or doctrine.

I.   Peer Pressure And Loyalty (Galatians 2:11-16, Acts 15:36-41)

Peer pressure is a very powerful force, whether for good or for ill. We all want to be liked and accepted. Therefore, we are inclined to do things which we think will win the approval of those we want to accept us. Conversely, we will tend to avoid doing those things which will mark us as misfits or different from the group we want to be part of.

There was a case of peer pressure which almost split the early church. We're not certain whether it occurred before or after the Jerusalem Council but, some time or other, Peter visited Antioch of Syria. The church at Antioch was an integrated church. Jews and Gentiles got along together in unity. They fellowshipped and ate together as one body.

Peter joined right in and everything went well until some men showed up from James in Jerusalem. When they arrived, Peter began to distance himself from the Gentile converts. Unfortunately, his example influenced the other Jewish members of the church, who started to do the same thing. It got so bad that even Barnabas, one of the men who had been instrumental in building the church up to what it was, joined in (Galatians 2:13).

That was the last straw for Paul. He publicly confronted Peter with his hypocrisy and got the church on an even keel again. To his credit, Peter accepted the correction. As far as we know, this was his last moral lapse. Even more to his credit he did not hold Paul's calling him on the carpet against him. Years later, Peter was able to describe Paul as his "dear brother" (2 Peter 3:15).

> **Question:** Does our behavior change depending on who is watching? Do we act differently when someone from a particular church, or when a particular leader, is present? Do we put a higher priority on impressing someone than doing what's right? Are we more concerned about our reputation than what is good for the church as a whole? Are we open to correction? Do we hold grudges against those who correct us?

Another point of friction came to a head at Antioch. Paul suggested to Barnabas that they go and visit the churches they had planted to see how they were getting along (Acts 15:36). That sounded good to Barnabas, but he wanted to take John-Mark along again. Paul adamantly opposed the idea because John-Mark had deserted them on their prior journey. Also, though this is speculation, if John-Mark's report to Jerusalem was partially responsible for precipitating the crisis about whether Gentiles had to obey the Mosaic Law, it's understandable why Paul would be hesitant to take him along again.

On the other hand, Barnabas was a man who looked beyond people's past and saw their potential. I can imagine him saying to Paul, "I was the man who saw what you could become in spite of your past. I befriended you and gave you a chance when no one else would. I'm the guy who brought you into this ministry. I'm the one who trained and mentored you. On the basis of what I did for you, you, of all people, ought to be willing to give a second chance to someone else!"

Unfortunately, Paul and Barnabas could not see eye-to-eye on this. The argument escalated to the point where they parted company

(Acts 15:39). It was tragic that two people, both of whom were wholeheartedly trying to serve the Lord, could no longer work together. God was able to bring much good out of the situation, but one wonders what might have happened if the rift had not taken place. Who was at fault?

> Scripture does not assign blame and we should be slow to assign it where Scripture does not. However, it's hard not to view Paul as ungracious in the way he treated John-Mark. There is a possible, implied criticism of Barnabas as well. The account says that "...Paul chose Silas and left, commended by the brothers to the grace of the Lord." (Acts 15:40 NIV) It merely records that "...Barnabas took Mark and sailed for Cyprus..." (Acts 15:39 NIV) In other words, it seems that Paul and Silas had the blessing of the church for their missionary tour, while Barnabas and Mark may not have.

Whether Barnabas went with the blessing of the church or not, his confidence in John-Mark was not misplaced. After maturing and seasoning under Barnabas' mentoring, he became an outstanding figure in the early church. Among other things, we owe the Gospel of Mark to him.

It's also significant that, as mentioned in the previous chapter, Paul and John-Mark were able to work together in the future. It also seems that Paul and Barnabas healed the rift between them, too. Paul mentions Barnabas in 1 Corinthians 9:6. It is obvious that Paul was familiar with Barnabas' work and approved of it.

II.   All Things To All Men (Acts 16:1-5)

Paul and Silas traveled overland to the churches he and Barnabas had planted earlier in Derbe and Lystra. It spite of Paul's break with Barnabas, it seems that he had learned from Barnabas' example. In Lystra he saw a young man with outstanding potential and recruited him to be part of the team. Timothy proved not only to be a tremendous help to Paul, but a gifted evangelist in his own right.

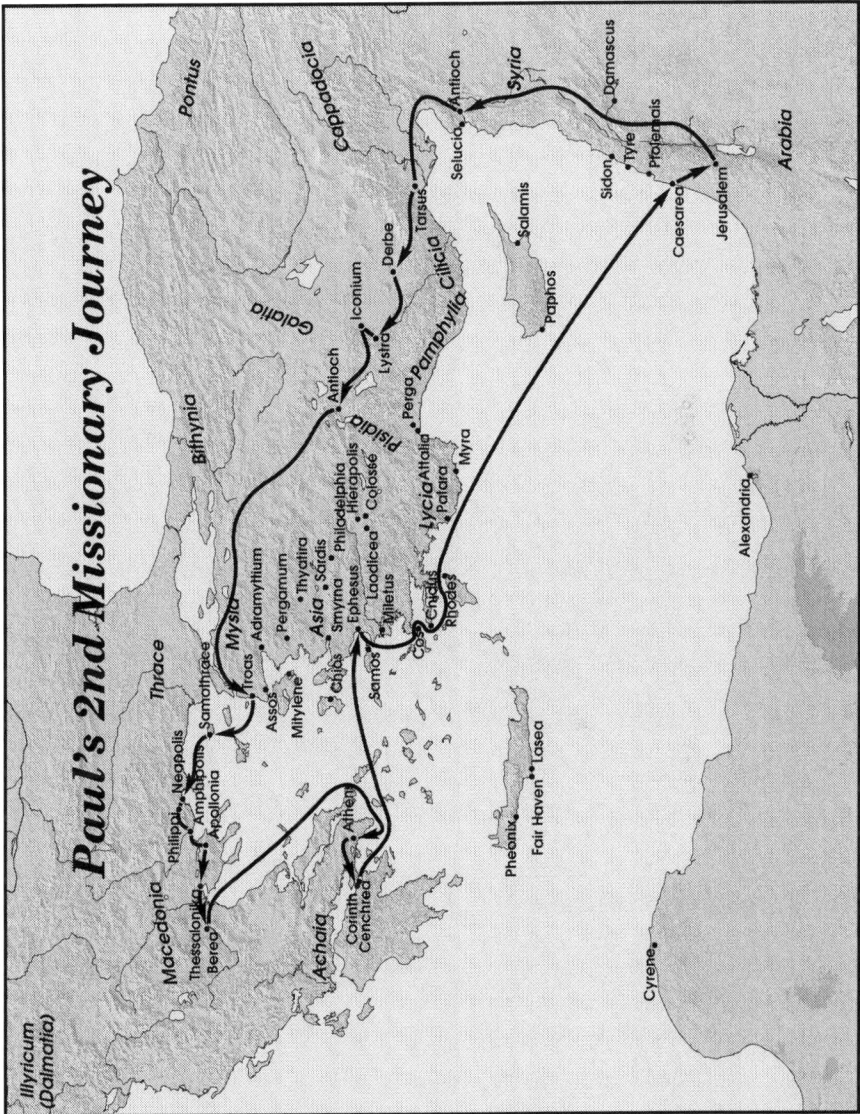

Paul's 2nd Missionary Journey

Before taking him along, however, Paul had Timothy circumcised. Why do that? Wasn't it inconsistent with, or a contradiction of, Paul's teaching that we are saved by faith and not by observing the Law of Moses? Why circumcise Timothy, while not doing it to Titus?

No, it was not a contradiction. There was another principle at work. Titus was a Gentile. After the Jerusalem Council, nobody (except the false teachers) expected Gentiles to be circumcised. But Timothy's mother was a Jewess. In the thinking of the Jewish people, that made Timothy a Jew, too. For a Jew to be uncircumcised was unthinkable. Though Paul was an Apostle to the Gentiles, he still tried to win Jews as well. For Timothy to remain uncircumcised would have destroyed all credibility among Jews and would have made evangelizing among them almost impossible. So, Paul circumcised him. It was a practical application of a principle Paul articulated in his letter to the Corinthians. As far as possible, he removed cultural and other artificial barriers so that he could win people to Christ (see 1 Corinthians 9:19-22).

Question: It says a lot about Timothy that he was willing to go through a very painful, humiliating and, in those days, dangerous, operation in order not to become a stumbling-block to the people they were trying to introduce to Christ. How committed are we? What are we willing to do, or to sacrifice, so others can hear the Gospel?

III.   Jail Ministry (Acts 16:11-40)

After visiting the churches in Galatia and delivering the decision reached at the Jerusalem Council, Paul and his companions tried to go west into the Roman province of Asia. The Holy Spirit would not allow them to go there (Acts 16:6). Since the way west was blocked, they next tried to go north into Bithynia. Again, the Spirit would not allow them to go there. So, they ended up going north-west, between the two forbidden territories.

When they got to Troas, Paul had a vision in which a man begged him to come to Macedonia (Acts 16:8-9). Believing this was a directive from God, he and his companions sailed for Macedonia. Upon arriving, they traveled to Philippi. Based on the use of the word 'we' in the text, it seems that Luke had joined the mission at Troas. What is significant about this journey is that, up till now, all of Paul's ministry had been in the Middle East or Asia Minor. Now, for the first time, he crossed over into Europe.

> **Note:** Contrary to what you might have heard, this was not the first time the Gospel reached Europe. Among those who heard the Gospel on the day of Pentecost were visitors from Rome (Acts 2:10-11). Apparently, some of them were converted and established the church in Rome not long afterwards. Aquila and his wife Priscilla had recently come from Italy before Paul met them in Corinth, and apparently were already Christians (Acts 18:1-3). Later, when Paul was taken to Rome to stand trial, he met believers in Puteoli and Rome (Acts 28:13-15). Further, Paul wrote his letter to the church in Rome a few years before he got there in person (Romans 1:8-13). While this was not the first time the Gospel reached Europe, it was the first time an Apostle had reached there.

In Philippi, on the Sabbath, Paul and his companions went to a place of prayer down by the river, presumably, because there wasn't any synagogue. Paul preached the Gospel to the women gathered there. As a result, a business woman named Lydia, and her whole household, came to Christ. She insisted that Paul use her house as his base of operations in Philippi.

They spent some time in Philippi, and things were going well until Paul's ministry touched some people in the pocketbook. He cast a demon out of a slave girl who had the ability to tell fortunes. Far from being grateful that the girl had been healed, her owners were furious that they could no longer make money off her. They had Paul and Silas arrested under a false charge, flogged and jailed.

Sleep was probably impossible, not only because of the pain but, because they were fastened in stocks. While most of us would probably have been moaning and feeling sorry for ourselves, Paul and Silas spent the time praying and singing hymns while the other prisoners listened (Acts 16:25). (Think of this as the first jail ministry!) As a result of their witness, none of the prisoners ran away when an earthquake broke the jail open and loosened everyone's chains. This so impressed the jailer than he and his household listened to the Gospel and were converted.

> **Question:** How would we use our time if we were thrown in jail? What would the effect of our witness be?

In the morning the magistrates told the jailer to release Paul and Silas. But Paul refused to go quietly. For the first time, he stood on his rights as a Roman citizen and forced the magistrates to eat humble pie. The magistrates asked him and Silas to leave Philippi. They did so, but in their own time. They first went back to Lydia's house and encouraged the brothers before they left.

IV.   True Nobility (Acts 17:1-15)

Thessalonica was the next place they ministered. A large number of people responded to the Gospel. However, the Jews became jealous and stirred up a mob against them. When the mob were unable to locate Paul and Silas, they dragged Jason and some of the other converts before the city officials. The officials made these men post bond before they let them go. Presumably, the bond was a pledge that Paul and Silas would leave town and stay away in the future. In other words, if Paul and Silas had remained in Thessalonica, or come back, it would have caused a major financial loss to the Christians there.

The brothers sent Paul and Silas on to Berea. In Berea they encountered people whom the account describes as "more noble" than the Thessalonians (Acts 17:11). In this context, what does it mean to be noble?

> It means to have a superior character. Nobility, in this sense, might be recognized by actions, but it is not good or right actions, themselves, which make one noble. It is the good, true, honest and upright character which produces good and right actions that makes a person noble. Jesus said, "No good tree bears bad fruit, nor does a bad tree bear good fruit. Each tree is recognized by its own fruit. People do not pick figs from thornbushes, or grapes from briers. The good man brings good things out of the good stored up in his heart, and

the evil man brings evil things out of the evil stored up in his heart. For out of the overflow of his heart his mouth speaks." (Luke 6:43-45 NIV) As an example of true nobility, consider the wife Proverbs 31:10-31 describes. It is not her works, per se, which make her noble, but the character which produces what she does.

What was it that demonstrated the noble character of the Bereans?

1) They received the message of the Gospel with great eagerness. They were not cynical or looking for fault. They weren't looking for an excuse to reject the message. They had the attitude of wanting to hear and to know what God says. They didn't deny the need to change.

2) They examined the Scriptures to see if what they heard was true. In spite of their eagerness to hear and accept what Paul said, they were not gullible. They had an objective standard by which to measure what they heard, and they used that standard to verify Paul's message. It's also worth noticing that Paul was not offended or intimidated by this. We should welcome it when people look into the Word for themselves to check what we say.

Question: Based on the example of the Bereans, how noble are we? Do we have the same character traits as they did?

The Jews in Thessalonica demonstrated that they were not as noble as the people in Berea, because when they heard that Paul was preaching in Berea, they came down and stirred up the crowd against him (Acts 17:13). As a result, Paul had to leave town again. Brothers from Berea escorted him down to Athens (Acts 17:15).

V.   Confrontation With Philosophy And Culture (Acts 17:16-18:22)

In Athens Paul faced a new set of challenges.

1) For the first time since Barnabas had brought him from Tarsus, Paul was alone. His support group was absent. This, no doubt contributed to his sense of isolation and loneliness.

Though Timothy apparently joined Paul in Athens, Paul sent him, almost immediately, back to Thessalonica to see how the Christians there were doing. (Compare Acts 17:15 and 1 Thessalonians 3:1-2.)

2) Though Paul had encountered idolatry before (for example at Lystra where they wanted to sacrifice to him), it had never before been so pervasive and "in your face". He was distressed to see the city full of idols (Acts 17:16).

3) While Paul was not persecuted in Athens, it must have been almost worse to be greeted by indifference. Even worse, was to have the Gospel treated as just another philosophy or quaint idea. The Athenians liked to talk about new things but seldom actually applied what they heard (Acts 17:21).

4) Always before, people had taken Paul's message seriously, though they had not always welcomed it. In Athens he encountered philosophers who dismissed him and the Gospel, at best, as incomprehensible (Acts 17:18).

Eventually, Paul got the opportunity to address a meeting of the Areopagus – a council of former rulers of the city. When preaching to Jews, Paul tried to develop rapport with them by reciting Jewish history and showing how Jesus fulfilled the hopes and desires of the Israelites. Before this Gentile audience, he talked about their common humanity and how something in the human spirit reaches out to the Creator. While a few people believed, others mocked when Paul mentioned the resurrection of the dead (Acts 17:32). Not long after this, Paul left and went to Corinth.

If the major challenge in Athens was Greek philosophy, the major challenge in Corinth would prove to be Roman culture. (At this stage of history, Corinth had been rebuilt and resettled as a Roman colony.) In another sense, however, Paul was back on familiar ground – the Gentiles were receptive to the Gospel while Jewish opposition was strong.

In Corinth, Paul received help from an unexpected source. He met Aquila and Priscilla, a Jewish husband and wife who had been expelled from Rome (Acts 18:2). It is highly likely that they were already Christians by the time Paul met them. If so, they must have been a great encouragement to him. They also provided employment and a place to stay (Acts 18:3). From this we can deduce that Paul had reached the end of whatever funds the Christians from Berea had given him when they brought him to Athens.

Silas and Timothy caught up with Paul in Corinth. After they came, Paul devoted full time to evangelism (Acts 18:5). Presumably, they brought funds from Macedonia so he could, or they found work in Corinth.

Paul stayed in Corinth for a year and a half (Acts 18:11). Many were baptized into Christ during this time (Acts 18:8). One of the converts was Crispus, the synagogue ruler. In spite of his conversion, Jewish opposition became so fierce that Paul had to abandon the synagogue altogether (Acts 18:7).

At some point, the Jews tried to bring legal action against Paul. However, the Roman proconsul, Gallio, dismissed the case as a waste of the court's time (Acts 18:14-16). Sosthenes had replaced Crispus as synagogue leader and, presumably, it was he who instigated the lawsuit. When Gallio ejected the Jews from court, they turned on Sosthenes and beat him up (Acts 18:17).

After some time, Paul left Corinth to return to Antioch. On the way he made a brief visit to Ephesus, where he left Aquila and Priscilla (Acts 18:19-20). From there he sailed to Caesarea. Then he traveled to Antioch (Acts 18:22).

VII.   Two Letters To The Thessalonians

While Paul was in Corinth he wrote two letters to the believers in Thessalonica. Remember that Paul had been forced to leave there after only a short time. He could not return without violating the bond Jason and the other Christians posted. Not only had Paul not had time to give the new converts much teaching, the church suffered persecution. Naturally, he was worried about whether the Christians remained faithful.

From Athens, Paul sent Timothy back to Thessalonica to check up on the situation (1 Thessalonians 3:1-3). Timothy brought back an encouraging report (1 Thessalonians 3:6). The new converts remained faithful and remembered Paul with affection. However, the Christians had some lifestyle problems and were confused about the resurrection.

Paul wrote his first letter to address these issues. He praised the believers for their faith in the face of persecution. He reminded them of his own example of righteous living. He dealt with the specific problem of sexual immorality. He talked about the need to earn a living.

The believers in Thessalonica apparently had the idea that only those who were still alive when Christ returned would live with Him forever. They did not understand that the dead would rise. So, Paul instructed them about the resurrection and that we will be reunited with those who have died in Christ before us.

Unfortunately, somebody apparently forged a letter in Paul's name claiming that the resurrection had already taken place (2 Thessalonians 2:1-2). Naturally, this upset the Christians in Thessalonica. Others, got the notion that Christ's return was just around the corner and so it was pointless to go to work.

Paul addressed both of these problems in his second letter. He pointed out that certain things had to happen before Christ's coming. Therefore, His return was not eminent. He also restated, but much more forcefully, the necessity for people to work and earn an honest living. If a person wouldn't work, then he could go hungry (2 Thessalonians 3:10).

In addition to instruction and admonition, Paul also gave comfort and reassurance. Remember that this church was suffering persecution. Paul reminded them of the reward they would receive at Christ's coming (2 Thessalonians 1:5, 10). He also assured them that God is just and He would repay their persecutors (2 Thessalonians 1:6-9).

Question: Where does this leave us? Do we believe in the resurrection of the dead? Are we looking forward to Christ's return? Is our lifestyle holy? Do we believe that God is just and that He will reward us for our faith and perseverance in trials and hardship? Do we have an honest occupation or do we have the attitude that the world owes us a living?

ജ്യഭ

Strengthening the Churches

Introduction: There is nothing easy about evangelism and missionary work. In city after city, Paul and his companions encountered severe opposition and persecution from unbelievers. But preaching is only one part of the missionary's task. Part of the job is teaching, training and nurturing new believers after their conversion.

Wherever he went, Paul organized the new believers into congregations. He also appointed Elders in each congregation to oversee and shepherd the believers. However, this did not mean that Paul's responsibilities were at an end. The new congregations still had problems. They still needed direction. They still needed teaching – remember that most of the New Testament had not yet been written. All of this put a tremendous strain on Paul. In 2 Corinthians 11:22-33, Paul gives a catalog of the sufferings he endured for Christ. Right in the middle of it he says, "Besides everything else, I face daily the pressure of my concern for all the churches." (2 Corinthians 11:28 NIV)

I.   Misconceptions (Acts 18:23-19:20)

After spending some time at Antioch of Syria, Paul's concern for the churches sent him on another tour of the congregations he had helped establish (Acts 18:23). Presumably, this included the congregations at Derbe, Lystra, Iconium and Antioch of Pisidia.

Acts, chapters 18 and 19 give us a glimpse of the kinds of misconceptions the early church had to deal with. The same misconceptions are still with us.

1) Inadequate or incomplete information (Acts 18:24-28).

While Paul was in the interior of Asia Minor, a man by name of Apollos arrived at Ephesus. Apollos had a lot going for him. He was educated. He knew the Scriptures. His knowledge about Jesus, as far as it went, was accurate. He was a good debater (Acts 18:28). It's probable that he was an eloquent speaker, in contrast to Paul, who was not (see

2 Corinthians 11:6). It is certain that some people preferred him to Paul (see 1 Corinthians 1:12).

His problem was that his information was incomplete. He only knew about the baptism of John. It seems that though he accepted Jesus as the Messiah on the basis of John's testimony, he apparently was ignorant of Jesus' ministry and the Gospel. When Aquila and Priscilla heard him and realized the problem, they invited him home and taught him more adequately.

It must have taken some courage for a businessman and his wife to presume to correct a highly educated and gifted orator. However, in spite of his background and social position, Apollos showed the humility of a true disciple. He was not too proud to admit that he needed to learn. He was willing to learn from people who did not have his educational background. Because of his willingness to listen and learn, the church gained a powerful apologist.

2) Incomplete faith (Acts 19:1-7).

Apollos left Ephesus with the endorsement and commendation of the church, and traveled to Corinth. While he was there, Paul traveled overland to Ephesus. When he arrived, he met some disciples whose characters apparently didn't match their claim of discipleship. Presumably, no fruit of the Spirit was evident (see Galatians 5:22-24). This prompted Paul to ask whether they had received the Holy Spirit at all. When these disciples professed total ignorance of the Spirit, Paul asked about their baptism. Upon hearing that they had received John's baptism, Paul told them about Jesus. Then, he baptized them into the name of Jesus. After their baptism, these disciples received some of the supernatural gifts of the Spirit through the laying on of Paul's hands.

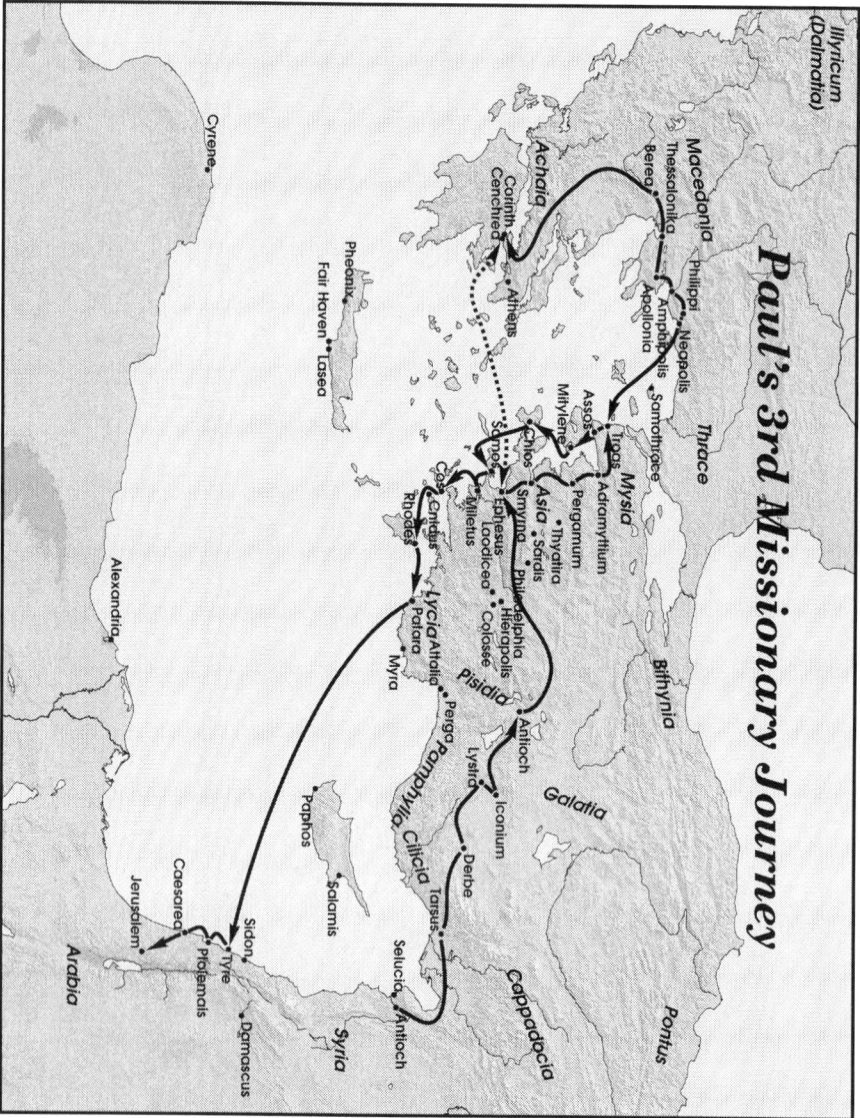

Paul's 3rd Missionary Journey

Tangent: Both Apollos and this group of disciples only knew of John's baptism. Both were given further teaching. Yet, these disciples were baptized into Christ, while Apollos was not. Why the difference?

The purpose of John's ministry was to prepare the way for Jesus and point people to Him. When people accepted Jesus as the Christ as a result of John's testimony, they repented of their sins and were baptized by him, their baptism was taken as equivalent to Christian baptism. After Pentecost, the Holy Spirit became active in their lives. They did not need to be baptized again upon receiving more information about Christ.

This was not the case, however, in the disciples Paul met at Ephesus. John's baptism did not have the intended result. Since, their baptism did not proceed to faith in Christ, it was based on false premises. In fact, their allegiance to John can be seen as opposition to faith in Christ. Paul had to preach the Gospel to them just as he would to anyone else. When they believed as a result of hearing the Gospel, they were baptized into Christ. This was not a re-baptism since their first one was not legitimate.

3) Imitation (Acts 19:11-17).

Sometimes there are those who want to profit by copying or imitating the church. They want to use the power of Christ without making a commitment to Him. This can be a problem because outsiders are not always able to tell the fake from the legitimate.

While in Ephesus, Paul performed many miracles. Some Jewish exorcists tried to imitate this by using Jesus' name to drive out a demon. Their attempt backfired. The demon gave these men a thrashing. As a result, instead of the activities of these men bringing discredit on the church, the people honored Jesus' name (Acts 19:17).

4) Syncretism (Acts 19:19-20).

A related problem is that of syncretism. People try to add Christianity to their existing belief system or practices. For example, Hindus will try to add Christ as another god to their existing pantheon.

However, faith in Christ is exclusive. It is not compatible with other belief systems. We must choose one or the other. One effect of the incident with the exorcists was that people realized they had to make a choice. Many decided to follow Christ exclusively and burned their magic books (Acts 19:19). The monetary value of the books (the equivalent of roughly 136 years' wages) proved the sincerity of their commitment.

II.   The First Letter To The Corinthian Church

Sometime during the three years he spent at Ephesus, Paul received a report about conditions in the church at Corinth. He heard that there were deep divisions in the church. There was also gross sexual immorality. The Christians were also taking each other to court.

In addition to these issues, the church wrote Paul asking for instructions about various problems. They had questions about marriage, eating food sacrificed to idols, head coverings, the Lord's Supper, spiritual gifts and the resurrection.

The basic problem in Corinth was spiritual immaturity and a lack of love. So, in addition to addressing the specific problems and issues in his letter, Paul also tried to deal with the root cause of the problems. Chapter 13 of the letter, on the subject of love, is one of the most well-known of all Paul's writings. Paul also gave instructions for collecting the gift he wanted to take to Jerusalem (1 Corinthians 16:1-4).

At some point Paul also made a quick trip to Corinth. We infer this from Paul's statements in his second letter that he was coming for a third visit (see 2 Corinthians 12:14, 13:1). Though the chronology is not clear, it's probable that this visit took place before Paul wrote 1ˢᵗ Corinthians. From his reference to another "painful visit" (2 Corinthians 2:1) we infer that the visit was not a total success. Not only did it not solve the problems, the two letters we have make it clear that the Corinthians challenged Paul's authority (for example see 1 Corinthians 9:3 and context).

III.   Riot

Paul made plans to pay another visit to Corinth and Macedonia. Before he could leave, though, there was a serious development at Ephesus. So many people throughout the province of Asia had become Christians, that the tourist trade to the temple of Artemis at Ephesus fell off. That had an impact on the sale of silver shrines and statues of the goddess. In protest, the trade guild incited a riot. The danger of violence to Paul was so great that the disciples prevented him from trying to address the crowd. Even some of the provincial officials told him not to attempt it (Acts 19:30-31). It was several hours before the city clerk was able to calm and disperse the crowd.

IV.   To Macedonia (Acts 19:21-22, 20:1-2)

Paul had originally intended to visit Corinth on his way to Macedonia (2 Corinthians 1:16). However, because of conditions at Corinth, he decided that it would be better to switch the itinerary and visit Macedonia first. This change of plans opened him up to further accusations from the Corinthians.

On his way to Macedonia, Paul stopped at Troas. Even though he had an opportunity for effective ministry there, Paul did not stay long. The reason was that he had expected to meet up with Titus at Troas (2 Corinthians 2:13). Titus had apparently delivered the first letter and Paul was anxious to hear how the church at Corinth had received it. Since Titus was not at Troas, Paul decided to intercept him in Macedonia.

V.   The Second Corinthian Letter

After meeting Titus in Macedonia, and hearing his report on conditions in Corinth, Paul wrote a second letter to the Corinthians. Titus was able to report that the first letter had had some positive effects. Though the church still had some issues with Paul, they were concerned about him (2 Corinthians 7:7). The church had disciplined one of the sex offenders and now needed instruction on restoring him. Paul also defended his ministry and apostolic authority, gave additional teaching on the New Covenant and encouraged the believers at Corinth to be generous in the offering for the church at Jerusalem. He also warned them that, if necessary, he would not hesitate to use his apostolic authority to discipline them during his coming visit.

VI.   The Letter To The Romans

Though we have few details, it's possible that Paul spent as long as a year in Macedonia. It's probable that during this period, either he or his companions took the Gospel northwest, into the territory of Illyricum (Romans 15:19). After traveling through Macedonia, Paul spent three months in Corinth (Acts 20:3). During this time he wrote a letter to the church at Rome.

Romans is the most systematic and comprehensive explanation of the Gospel and the process of salvation we have. The first 11 chapters discuss the theology of salvation. The last 4 chapters contain practical instructions on how to live in Christ.

Why would Paul need to discuss salvation so thoroughly with people who were already in the faith? We cannot know for sure, but the Christians in Rome had never had the benefit of apostolic teaching. Though they had come to faith in Christ, it's likely that they had never been told, or understood, the true nature of the Gospel.

VII.   On To Jerusalem (Acts 20:3-21:16)

Paul intended to sail directly from Greece to Syria (Acts 20:3). However, because of a plot on his life, he decided to go back through Macedonia and sail from there. By this time he had collected the offering for the church at Jerusalem and the representatives of the contributing churches had gathered at Corinth. So, the return through Macedonia must have meant a great deal of extra and duplicated travel for these men.

In spite of the short time Paul spent there while traveling to Macedonia a year earlier, there was a thriving church at Troas. Paul and his companions met with the church to take the Lord's Supper

(Acts 20:7). This is the first definitive statement we have that the church met on the first day of the week.

While there, Paul talked all night. Around midnight a young man went to sleep and fell from a window to his death. Paul raised him from the dead, then continued talking till daybreak.

From Troas, Paul traveled to Miletus. There he met with the Elders from Ephesus. He reminded them of how he had set them an example while he ministered to them. He warned them about the need to guard both themselves and the church against apostasy. He told them of the journey he was making to Jerusalem and that the Spirit was warning him of prison and the hardships he was going to have to face. After praying with them, Paul and his companions sailed on to Syria.

They landed at Tyre where the Christians urged Paul not to go to Jerusalem. The Christians at Caesarea did the same after the prophet Agabus predicted that Paul would be bound and handed over to the Gentiles. However, Paul would not be dissuaded and went on to Jerusalem.

Tangent: Did Paul disobey the Holy Spirit in going to Jerusalem? It's not entirely clear. Acts 21:4 says that the disciples at Tyre urged Paul through the Spirit not to go to Jerusalem. Yet, in Acts 20:22 Paul told the Ephesian Elders that the Spirit was compelling him to go. Acts 21:4 definitely refers to the Holy Spirit. Acts 20:22 could refer to the Holy Spirit, or to Paul's own spirit. Likewise, Acts 19:21 literally says, "Paul purposed in the spirit." This may refer to Paul's own spirit, as interpreted the NIV and many other translations, or it could be understood as the Holy Spirit directing Paul to go to Jerusalem. One thing is certain. Paul received multiple warnings that he would face imprisonment if he went to Jerusalem. Whether the Spirit intended the warnings to prevent Paul going to Jerusalem, or whether the Spirit merely prepared him for the ordeal ahead, is open to interpretation.

Question: Would we be willing to go ahead with a task God had given us if we knew for certain that we would be jailed as a result?

೫೦೦೪

Put on Ice

Introduction: At the end of his third evangelistic tour, Paul and his companions went to Jerusalem. The reason was to deliver a large offering which Paul had collected from the Gentile churches for the Christians in Judea.

What was the purpose of this offering? On a personal level, though Scripture does not say so, Paul may still have felt an obligation to make reparations for the persecution he had brought upon the church years earlier. Though forgiven, he may still have felt a responsibility to help the families of those he had killed.

Another reason was that the churches in Jerusalem and Judea were poor. There were at least three reasons for their poverty.

> 1) Undoubtedly many of the pilgrims who had come to Jerusalem to celebrate the festival of Pentecost and heard Peter's sermon had stayed to receive additional teaching and instruction after their conversion, instead of immediately returning home. This would have put a strain on the resources of the local believers. Acts 2:45 records that the believers sold their possessions in order to meet the needs of others.

> 2) The Jerusalem church had suffered several waves of persecution. The persecution which broke out after Stephen was stoned to death was so severe that it scattered everyone except the Apostles (Acts 8:1). No doubt this had a huge impact on people's incomes and careers.

> 3) They had also experienced famine (Acts 11:28).

> For all these reasons, the church in Jerusalem probably needed some financial help.

Most importantly, however, Paul wanted to use this offering as a means to demonstrate unity between the Gentile and Jewish branches of Christianity. On the one hand, Paul felt that the Gentiles were in debt to the Jewish Christians because the Gentiles shared in the Jews' spiritual blessings (Romans 15:26-27). On the other hand, by accepting the offering, the Jewish Christians would demonstrate that they also accepted the Gentile Christians as brothers in Christ (2 Corinthians 9:12-14).

Unfortunately, there was also danger involved in this act of generosity and reconciliation. In city after city, the Holy Spirit explicitly warned Paul that he faced imprisonment by going to Jerusalem (Acts 20:23, 21:10-11). Whether Paul disobeyed the Spirit by going to Jerusalem anyway is open to debate. Assuming that he did disobey may explain what followed. It may be one reason why Paul had to spend the next two years languishing in prison in Caesarea.

I.   Public-Relations Problem (Acts 21:17-26)

Paul was anxious that the Jerusalem church accept the offering he brought and, thus, demonstrate unity with the Gentile churches. But his coming with the offering also created a dilemma for the Jerusalem church. Nationalist feelings were on the rise among the Jewish people. A decade later these feelings would break out in open revolt against the Romans – ultimately leading to the destruction of the Temple. In addition to the nationalist movement in Jewish society, many in the church were very zealous for the Law of Moses (Acts 21:20).

The church's dilemma was this: How could they, on the one hand, identify with the Gentile churches by accepting their offering, without antagonizing their own countrymen and many even within the church? On the other hand, how could they reassure their own people that they were not abandoning their Jewish identity without raising fresh concerns among the Gentile believers about the necessity to keep the Law?

They came up with an ingenious solution to this public-relations problem.

> 1) They welcomed the delegation warmly (Acts 21:17) and praised God upon hearing Paul's report about what God was doing among the Gentiles (Acts 21:20).

2) They asked Paul to pay the expenses for some men among their number who had made a Nazirite vow. This would defuse the perception that Paul taught Jews to repudiate the Law as paying someone's expenses was viewed, not only as an act of piety, but as proclaiming oneness with the Jewish people (Expositor's Bible Commentary, Volume 9, Frank E. Gaebelein general editor, Zondervan, 1981, p. 520).

3) They reaffirmed the decision of the Jerusalem Council (Acts 21:25). This must have been very reassuring to the Gentile believers who accompanied Paul.

II.   For The Hope Of The Resurrection (Acts 21:27-23:11)

While the church was able to defuse its internal public-relations problem, their course of action backfired among the pilgrims who came to Jerusalem for the festivals. Paul's going to the Temple gave his enemies from the province of Asia the opportunity to accuse him of defiling it. They saw Paul and Trophimus together and assumed that Paul brought him into the Temple (Acts 21:29).

On the basis of this false assumption, these men stirred up the whole crowd. They dragged Paul out of the Temple proper to the Court of Gentiles and tried to kill him. The uproar spread to the whole city. When the Roman commander heard what was going on, he intervened by arresting Paul. He thought that Paul was a known terrorist who had led a previous revolt (Acts 21:38). Paul disabused the commander of this notion and asked permission to speak to the crowd. The commander agreed, probably because he hadn't been able to find out what the crowd had against Paul, and was hoping that what Paul said would shed some light on the matter.

Paul told the crowd about his background and his conversion to Christ. They listened quietly until Paul said that God had commissioned him to go to the Gentiles (Acts 22:21-22). This set the crowd off again and the commander ordered Paul into the barracks.

The commander was still not any wiser about what accusations were being made against Paul, so he ordered him to be questioned under torture. Paul forestalled that by revealing his Roman citizenship.

This put the whole case in a different light. The commander, himself, could be in trouble for not following proper procedure (Acts 22:25-29).

Not only did the commander feel exposed to accusation, he still didn't know or understand what the charges against Paul were. If he held Paul unjustly, his own career was on the line. If he let Paul go, it would sour relations with the Jewish authorities. In an attempt to get to the bottom of the situation, he ordered the Sanhedrin to meet and brought Paul before it.

> **Note:** This was a special session of the Sanhedrin. It could not have met in its normal chamber within the Temple sanctuary, otherwise the commander, who was a Gentile, could not have entered. Similarly, the soldiers could not have entered to rescue Paul from the uproar which later ensued. Also, while the commander could order the Sanhedrin to meet, he could not preside over it or speak to it.

Paul began his defense by declaring his innocence (Acts 23:1). When the High Priest ordered someone to strike Paul for saying this, Paul lost his temper and verbally lashed out at the High Priest. When those standing near rebuked Paul for insulting the High Priest he apologized (Acts 23:5).

> **Tangent:** Paul said that he hadn't realized that the person who ordered him struck was the High Priest. How could this be since Paul had been brought up in Jerusalem and, at one time, had worked closely with the Jewish authorities to persecute the church? Remember that Paul had been out of the country for several years. In the meantime, there had been changes in the priesthood. It's likely that Paul was unacquainted with Ananias, the current High Priest, or did not recognize him. Also, since this was a special session of the Sanhedrin, apparently outside the Temple precincts, it's probable that the High Priest was not wearing his robes of office. The robes were not supposed to leave the Temple. Therefore, Paul couldn't have recognized the High Priest by his vestments. Paul reacted to the injustice of being struck and then apologized when he found out who had ordered it.

Lesson: We must still respect the office, even if the person filling the office is not worthy of respect. Injustice does not excuse disrespect or showing contempt. "…if you suffer for doing good and you endure it, this is commendable before God. To this you were called, because Christ suffered for you, leaving you an example, that you should follow in his steps. "He committed no sin, and no deceit was found in his mouth." When they hurled their insults at him, he did not retaliate; when he suffered, he made no threats. Instead, he entrusted himself to him who judges justly." (1 Peter 2:20-23 NIV)

> **Tangent:** The order to strike Paul, even though it was totally contrary to the Law and normal procedure, was in keeping with the character of Ananias. He was known for violence. According to Josephus, he also confiscated the tithes which were supposed to go to the ordinary priests and paid large bribes to the Romans (Antiquities XX, 205-207).

Probably realizing that he couldn't expect a fair hearing from this group, Paul changed tactics and pitted one faction of the assembly against another. He proclaimed that the reason he was on trial was for his belief in the resurrection of the dead. This switched the attention away from Paul, himself, and put it on a key doctrine. To acquit or to condemn Paul now involved theological concessions which neither faction was willing to grant. The argument became so heated that the Roman commander had to send in troops to extract Paul from the uproar.

Undoubtedly, this must have been a time of stress for Paul. He was in prison, with no formal charges filed. The future looked very uncertain. However, God encouraged him in a vision and let him know that he would testify in Rome (Acts 23:11).

III.   Plot And Counter-Plot (Acts 23:12-35)

The next move in the drama was about 40 men making a vow to kill Paul. They swore not to eat or drink until they assassinated him (Acts 23:12). Word of the plot reached one of Paul's relatives who warned the Roman commander.

To counter this plot, the commander immediately sent Paul to the Roman governor at Caesarea. To let a Roman citizen in his custody be murdered could have had serious repercussions. As an escort, he provided a large contingent of soldiers – perhaps as many as half the entire garrison at Jerusalem.

> **Note:** The Greek word (dexiolaboi) which the NIV translates "spearmen" (Acts 23:23) appears only here. It does not appear in any extant Greek literature until about the sixth century. Therefore, translators must guess at the meaning. The only thing which is certain is that it is a rendition into Greek of some term in the Roman army. Based on the composition of the word ("dexios" means right-handed), most translators feel that it probably refers to some kind of infantry. However, since speed was of the essence in getting Paul to Caesarea, it's possible that the word refers to re-mounts and pack animals for the cavalry.

Even though he kicked Paul's case up to a higher level, the commander still had a problem. What could he tell the governor? He still didn't understand what the fuss was all about and why the Jews were so intent on killing Paul. To simultaneously get himself off the hook and to cast his actions in the most favorable light, the commander resorted to stretching the truth. He first claimed to have rescued Paul after hearing that he was a Roman citizen. He then presented his action of sending Paul to the governor as a case of protective custody. In a sense, this was true. The question remains that if, as he wrote in his letter to the governor, the commander had found that there was no charge against Paul which merited keeping him in prison, why didn't he merely escort Paul out of town? Why turn him over to the governor at all? We cannot know for sure, but it's likely that the commander was covering his own backside. He wanted to wash his hands of the case in a way that would get him into the least trouble with either the Jewish authorities or the governor. He was concerned about self-preservation, rather than justice.

Tangent: What happened to the 40 men who vowed not to eat or drink until they killed Paul? Did they die of thirst when the commander took Paul out of their reach? It's not likely. The Jews at this time had concocted all sorts of contingencies or circumstances in which a vow no longer applied. Legalists are generally pretty good at figuring out how the law applies to everyone except themselves. However, God views things differently. Granted their vow was not for a legitimate purpose. But vows should not be taken lightly. "Guard your steps when you go to the house of God. Go near to listen rather than to offer the sacrifice of fools, who do not know that they do wrong. Do not be quick with your mouth, do not be hasty in your heart to utter anything before God. God is in heaven and you are on earth, so let your words be few. As a dream comes when there are many cares, so the speech of a fool when there are many words. When you make a vow to God, do not delay in fulfilling it. He has no pleasure in fools; fulfill your vow. It is better not to vow than to make a vow and not fulfill it. Do not let your mouth lead you into sin. And do not protest to the temple messenger, "My vow was a mistake." Why should God be angry at what you say and destroy the work of your hands?" (Ecclesiastes 5:1-6 NIV)

IV.   Bribes And Favors (Acts 24:1-26:32)

Felix, the Roman governor, decided to hear the case against Paul. When Ananias, the High Priest, and entourage arrived, the trial began. The prosecuting lawyer started off by flattering Felix with a blatant lie. Contrary to the lawyer's assertion, Felix's rule had hardly been marked by a long period of peace (Acts 24:2). In fact, Felix had a reputation for corruption and cruelty. Within two years his brutal methods would lead to a formal complaint against him in Rome and his recall.

The lawyer then proceeded to accuse Paul of stirring up riots all over the world (Acts 24:5). He also claimed that Paul had tried to desecrate the Temple (Acts 24:6).

In his defense, Paul pointed out that the wrong people were bringing the accusations against him. It was really some Jews from the province of Asia who had started the troubles. If they had an accusation against Paul, it should be they who brought charges before the governor. Further, if the governor cared to investigate, he would find that Paul had come to Jerusalem, not to stir up trouble but, on a mission of benevolence.

After listening to both sides, Felix deferred making a decision with the excuse that he wanted to hear what the commander in Jerusalem had to say (Acts 24:22). However, instead of making a decision, Felix continued to dither. He would send for Paul frequently, apparently fascinated, yet afraid of Paul's messages about righteousness, self-control and the judgment (Acts 24:24-26). His real motive, however, was to get a bribe (Acts 24:26). This went on for two years. Since a bribe was not forthcoming, and wanting to do the Jews a favor (possibly in the hopes that it would lesson the complaints against him) Felix left Paul for the next administration to deal with (Acts 24:27).

The new governor, Festus, naturally did not want to begin his administration by quarreling with the Jews. When they told him about Paul's case, he quickly arranged a hearing in Caesarea. The Jews asked him to move the trial to Jerusalem intending to kill Paul while on his way there (Acts 25:3). Wanting to do them a favor, Festus asked Paul if he would be willing to stand trial Jerusalem. Rather than face a kangaroo court in Jerusalem, Paul, as was his right as a Roman citizen, made a direct appeal to Caesar (Acts 25:11).

This put Festus in a dilemma. He could hardly refuse Paul's request to be sent to Rome. Yet, there were no solid charges against Paul to justify sending him there. Fortunately, King Agrippa was due to arrive in a few days. Festus decided to consult him about what to do.

Before Agrippa and his court, Paul again recounted his conversion to Christ. He then went on to proclaim the Gospel to the king. The response was, "Do you think that in such a short time you can persuade me to be a Christian?" (Acts 26:28 NIV) Paul replied that he wished that everyone who was listening would become what he was – except for the chains he wore.

Afterwards, while discussing the case among themselves, those who were at the trial all agreed that Paul had done nothing deserving imprisonment, much less death (Acts 26:31). Instead of setting him free, however, they were obligated to send Paul to Rome because of his appeal to Caesar. Bureaucracy triumphed over justice.

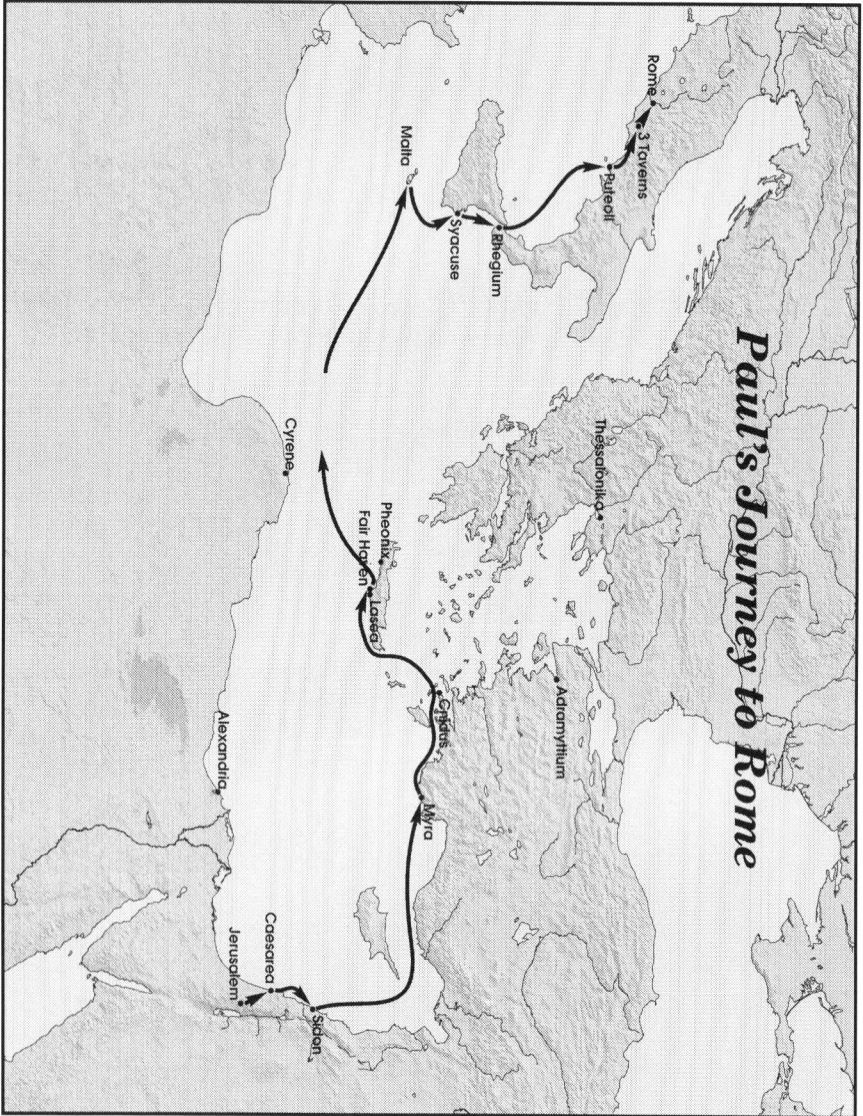

V.   To Rome (Acts 27:1-28:31)

In due course, a centurion named Julius who was responsible for taking several prisoners to Rome took custody of Paul. It's probable that Luke was on the voyage to Rome with Paul because the account in Acts uses the word "we" in describing what happened.

Due to unfavorable winds, the journey took much longer than anticipated. As a result, they had only traveled as far as Crete when it came time to seek a harbor in which to winter. In spite of Paul's warning, the ship's company decided to sail on in hopes of reaching a better anchorage. In the process they got caught in a hurricane which drove them far off course.

After two weeks of being driven by the storm, they were ship-wrecked on the island of Malta (Acts 28:1). There Paul won the hearts of the people by curing their sick.

After three months on Malta, they boarded another ship for Italy. The Christians in Rome heard that Paul was coming and met him at Three Taverns and, then, escorted him to Rome.

In Rome, Paul was allowed to rent a house. The authorities kept him under guard but allowed people to visit. Paul was free to preach the Gospel to those who came. The book of Acts ends by saying that Paul lived and preached under these conditions for two years.

VI.   New Testament Books

This and several previous chapters, emphasized the work of Paul. It's important to realize, however, that Paul did not work and move in a vacuum. Others were also working to spread the Gospel. Others were making important contributions to the life of the church. This becomes apparent when we consider the books of the New Testament.

1) Matthew

There is a great deal of controversy about when, and in what order the Gospel accounts were written. Many scholars think that Mark was the first to write and that Matthew and Luke borrowed from his material. However, it is also possible that

Matthew wrote first. As an eyewitness of Jesus' ministry it's not necessary for him to have borrowed from Mark. In any case, it's possible that Matthew wrote approximately during the time Paul was in prison at Caesarea.

Matthew wrote primarily for a Jewish audience. In the Gospel he emphasizes how Jesus fulfills Old Testament prophecy as the long awaited Messiah.

2) Luke/Acts

While it is possible that one reason Paul had to spend two years of his life languishing in prison in Caesarea was because he disobeyed the warnings of the Spirit not to go to Jerusalem, God still brought great good out of the situation. It is almost certain that Luke used this time to gather and compile the material he used to write the Gospel account which bears his name. He mentions written sources for some of his material (Luke 1:1-2) but it is probable that he also personally interviewed many of those who experienced or witnessed the events he recorded.

Luke's purpose in writing the Gospel was "so that you may know the certainty of the things you have been taught." (Luke 1:4 NIV) Luke wrote primarily for Gentiles. Through the Jesus film, which has been translated into more than 700 languages, the Gospel of Luke has probably reached a larger audience than any other Gospel.

The book of Acts is the sequel to the Gospel of Luke. As such it is the story of the continuation of the ministry of Christ after His ascension to heaven. Though the book records the actions of the more prominent Apostles, it is really Christ who is working through them by means of the Spirit.

3) Ephesians

While under house arrest in Rome, Paul wrote several letters. One of them was to the church in Ephesus. Actually, it's likely that he intended this letter as a circular letter to all the churches in the province of Asia.

In it Paul emphasizes unity in the church. Christ breaks down the walls which once divided Jew and Gentile. He then goes on to spell out the practical implications and applications of unity. It will show in what we believe. It will affect the way we communicate with each other. It will affect our lifestyle. It has a bearing on interpersonal relationships. He ends the letter urging people to put on the armor of God.

4) Colossians

About the same time, Paul also wrote the letter to the Colossians. The letter is similar in many ways to Ephesians, yet the emphasis is different. In Ephesians, the emphasis is on unity. In Colossians it is the supremacy of Christ (Colossians 1:18). Christ is head of the church. He is also Lord over the individual Christian.

This has implications for how we live. Christ is the standard, rather than tradition. We have died and have been raised with Christ. Therefore we must no longer submit to the standards and principles of the world. The world is guided by external rules, while the Christian is guided by love and the word of Christ.

5) Philippians

From Rome, Paul wrote a letter to the Christians at Philippi. He wrote it in response to a gift they sent him. The key teaching in this letter is having the same attitude as Christ. It is an attitude of humility and service. He mentions Timothy and Epaphroditus as examples of men who have the attitude of Christ.

One of the interesting things about this letter is that it gives us an indication of Paul's own spiritual growth. While writing to the Thessalonians, Paul was extremely worried that the troubles he and they were going through would cause them to lose their faith. In this letter Paul expresses a rock-solid faith that his hardships will actually cause the Gospel to advance. Whether he's acquitted or condemned at his trial, it will turn out for the best.

6) Philemon

During this same time, Paul wrote a personal letter to Philemon. In it he asked Philemon to forgive and accept back a runaway slave by the name of Onesimus whom Paul had met and brought to the Lord in Rome.

Paul also asked Philemon to prepare a guest room for him. Paul anticipated being acquitted at his trial and released from prison very shortly.

Faithful to the End

Introduction: The book of Acts ends with a description of Paul's ministry while under house arrest in Rome. This is the last section of narrative history of the Apostles' ministry we have in Scripture. However, it is not the last mention we have of what the Apostles did. There are several additional glimpses of their work in the letters and books they wrote after the completion of Acts.

I.   The Further Ministry of Paul

Paul's letters hint at several journeys which the book of Acts does not record. Most commentators agree that the Romans released Paul from prison shortly after the two years Acts, chapter 28 mentions. We know from Philippians 2:23-24 that Paul certainly expected the court to acquit and release him. This would have taken place about 61 or 62 AD. Where did Paul go after being released? We don't know enough details to establish a firm itinerary or chronology. Though we don't know the route he took or the timing, we can identify several places he went and ministered.

1) Spain – Romans 15:24, 28

Paul wrote to the believers at Rome that he intended to visit them on his way to Spain. Though Paul arrived in Rome as a prisoner rather than a free agent, it's likely that he was able to accomplish the ministry he intended to do in Rome even though he was under house arrest.

There is no statement in Scripture which says Paul was able to fulfill his other intention of going on to Spain. However, writings of early believers indicate that he did. Clement mentions that Paul went "...to the limits of the west..." (First Epistle of Clement to the Corinthians V. vii) Similarly, the Muratorian fragment says that Paul proceeded from Rome to Spain.

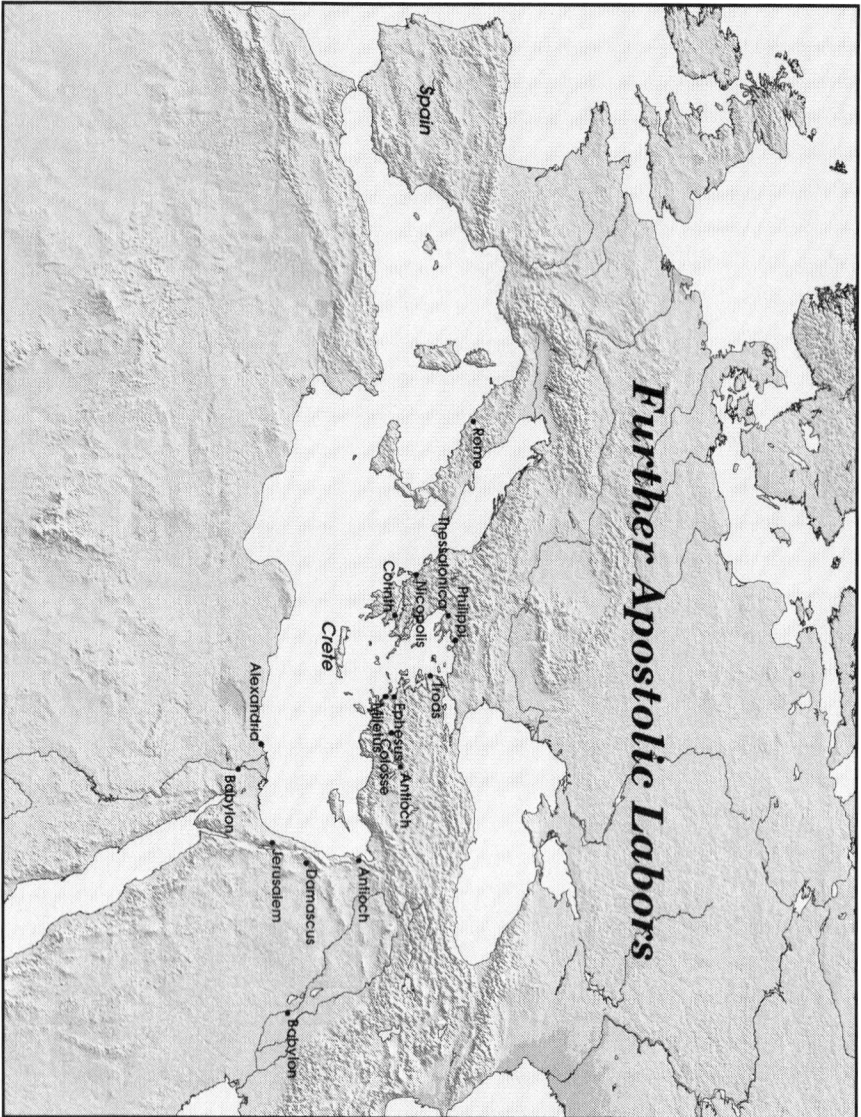

2) Crete – Titus 1:5

We know from Titus 1:5 that Paul also visited Crete. The ship carrying Paul to Rome as a prisoner touched at Crete, but he had had no opportunity to evangelize.

We do not know how long Paul stayed there on this trip, but apparently long enough to plant churches in several towns. He did not stay long enough, however, to fully establish the churches. He left the task of further teaching and the appointing of Elders to Titus, whom he left in Crete for that purpose.

3) Miletus – 2 Timothy 4:20

In addition to opening new works in Spain and Crete, Paul also revisited areas he had already evangelized in the Roman province of Asia. One of the places he visited was Miletus, where he had spoken to the Elders from Ephesus while on his way to Jerusalem with the offering for Jewish church (Acts 20:17-38).

The significant thing about this visit is that Paul left Trophimus there, sick. Since Paul had the gift of miraculous healing (Acts 19:11-12), why did he not heal Trophimus? We cannot know. But could it be that this is an indication that the supernatural gifts of the Spirit were already passing away? (For example, see 1 Corinthians 13:8.)

4) Colosse – Philemon 22

While in prison, Paul wrote to Philemon and asked him to prepare a guest room. Assuming Paul followed through on his intention, this means he traveled to Colosse.

Paul's statement to Philemon is one reason it is difficult to determine his itinerary with any certainty. From his letter, it sounds like Paul intended to arrive quite soon – else why would he ask Philemon to prepare a guest room? Yet, church tradition implies that Paul traveled to Spain directly from Rome. In other words, it may have been a year or two after his release from prison before Paul made it to Colosse.

Note: We deduce that Philemon lived at Colosse because Colossians 4:9 states that Onesimus, who was Philemon's slave, was one of them – meaning he was a member of the church at Colosse. It follows that the master (Philemon) would live in the same town as his slave.

5) Ephesus – 1 Timothy 1:3

Another stop on Paul's travels was Ephesus. 1 Timothy 1:3 specifically states that Paul left Timothy there.

How can we harmonize Paul's visit with his statement to the Elders from Ephesus in Acts 20, verses 25 and 38, that they would never see him again?

> There are at least two possibilities. One possibility is that the Elders Paul spoke to were no longer in the church. Paul predicted that false teachers would arise from within the group of Elders who would cause division (Acts 20:30). From Paul's instructions to Timothy it seems likely that this had already occurred. The Elders whom Paul talked to in Acts 20 had already separated themselves and left the faithful disciples without leaders. This may be one reason why Paul lists the qualifications for Elders in his first letter to Timothy. Timothy was left with the responsibility of rebuilding the church after the division occurred.

> The second possibility is that Paul stayed in Ephesus just long enough to see a few of the Christians and find out what the condition of the church was. He didn't meet with any of the Elders.

6) Macedonia, Philippi – 1 Timothy 1:3, Philippians 2:23-24

Paul left Ephesus and went on to Macedonia. We do not know where he visited while there, but it is likely that he went to Philippi. At least he told the Philippians that he intended to come.

7) Corinth – 2 Timothy 4:20

From Macedonia, Paul apparently traveled south into Greece. We do not know for certain that he visited Corinth, but his statement that Erastus stayed there may imply that he did.

8) Nicopolis – Titus 3:12

Paul told Titus that he intended to spend the winter at Nicopolis. Presumably he did so.

We don't know where it happened – possibly somewhere in Greece – but the government again arrested Paul and took him to Rome. To divert attention from himself and the shortcomings of his administration, the Emperor Nero blamed the Christians for subversion and the great fire at Rome in 64 AD. It is probably for this reason that he had Paul, one of the most prominent leaders of the Christian community, arrested and tried. Tradition says Paul died for the faith in about 67 AD. Since he was a Roman citizen, they beheaded him rather than throwing him to the beasts or inflicting one of the more gruesome deaths which other believers commonly suffered.

II.   Paul's Writings

In the period after his first imprisonment, Paul wrote at least three letters.

1) Titus

One of these letters was to Titus whom Paul left on Crete to finish organizing the churches there. This letter is extremely important because it contains a list of the character qualities Elders must have. It also talks about various aspects of daily living – the principles by which the followers of Christ should live their lives.

In Titus we also learn an important aspect of grace. It is grace which enables us to turn away from evil and live godly lives.

2) 1 Timothy

Paul left Timothy in Ephesus to deal with some serious doctrinal problems in the church. In the letter we know as

1st Timothy, Paul instructed him what to teach to various groups on various subjects. In this letter we have another list of qualifications for Elders. Paul also included instructions and advice to Timothy in regard to leadership and his personal life.

It is easy to get so immersed in church work and ministry that we forget the purpose for it all. The work can become an end in itself. In light of this, it is significant that Paul defines what the goal is: It is love (1 Timothy 1:5). Everything we do in the church needs to be evaluated by whether it will increase or detract from love.

3) 2 Timothy

After his arrest, Paul wrote another letter to Timothy. This is probably the last letter Paul wrote. In it he encourages Timothy to remain true to the faith – in the face of rising opposition and apostasy. Since Paul tells Timothy to do the work of an Evangelist (2 Timothy 4:5) in these two letters we gain important insights into what it means to be an Evangelist and the work of an Evangelist.

Commentators call the two letters to Timothy and the one to Titus 'Pastoral Letters' because they address the problems and issues of organizing and putting the church in order. In a way, this is really a misnomer, since in New Testament usage 'Shepherd' is another term or title for an Elder. Timothy (and presumably Titus, also) was not an Elder, but an Evangelist. Therefore, strictly speaking, these letters are 'pastoral' not in the sense that they teach Elders how to shepherd the flock, but in the sense that they instruct Evangelists how to appoint Shepherds for the flock.

III.   The Further Ministry of Peter

Our last glimpse of Peter was at Antioch of Syria, where Paul confronted him about his inconsistency in his relationship to Gentiles (Galatians 2:11-16). However, this was not the end of Peter's ministry. Though we have no record of his travels, it's probable that he visited many of the churches Paul established. At least his first letter is addressed to believers throughout the provinces of Asia Minor. We also know that there was a faction at Corinth who said that they followed Peter (1 Corinthians 1:12). That being the case, it's likely that Peter had been at Corinth.

One of the most intriguing references to Peter's ministry is in 1st Peter 5:13. He sends greetings from "she who is in Babylon." Peter is obviously referring to the church in Babylon. The question is, which Babylon? Many think that he wrote the letter from Rome and is using the name Babylon as an oblique reference to Rome. However, since he did not use any other oblique language for geographical places in the letter, it's quite possible that he is referring to an actual Babylon.

There was a Roman fort called Babylon, in Egypt just outside of what is now the city of Cairo. Some think that Peter wrote from there. In fact, one church tradition says that Peter and Mark evangelized in Egypt. Human nature being what it is, if Peter spent much time in Egypt it seems likely that the Egyptian church would claim Peter as its founder. Instead, they give that honor to Mark.

That leaves the Babylon on the Euphrates River. The tradition of the Eastern Church claims that Peter wrote the letter from this Babylon. Whether Peter reached Babylon or not, we know that the Gospel went far further east than Babylon during the apostolic period. (Thomas went at least as far as India.)

The authorities arrested Peter about the same time as Paul. They executed him as well during the Neronian persecution. Since he was not a Roman citizen, they crucified him instead instead of beheading him like Paul. This fulfilled the prophecy Christ made about his death (John 21:18-19). Tradition says that he told the executioners he was not worthy to die in the same way as his Lord and asked to be crucified upside down.

IV.   Peter's And Mark's Writings

Peter wrote two letters. The theme of the first one is how Christians should respond to persecution and suffering. In it he gives two universal principles which should govern all of our behavior: The first principle is to abstain from sinful desires (1 Peter 2:11). The second principle is to do good in all circumstances (1 Peter 2:12). He then gives several practical examples of how to apply these principles in specific areas.

Peter's intent in his second letter is to help people remember the basic concepts and principles of the faith (2 Peter 1:12-15). He points out that effectiveness in knowing Christ is a growth process. We are either moving forward, or we are losing ground. He goes on to say that our faith is based on both eyewitness testimony and the prophecy of Scripture. He also talks about false teachers and how to recognize them. He ends the letter by talking about the second coming of Christ and our hope of the new heaven and earth "the home of righteousness." (2 Peter 3:13)

Though we cannot be certain whether Peter was with Mark when Mark evangelized Egypt, it is quite certain that Peter and Mark did work together. In 2nd Peter 1:15, Peter remarks that he will make every effort to see that people will be able to remember his teaching after his death. If church tradition is accurate, one of the things Peter did was encourage Mark to write the Gospel which bears his name. According to tradition, Mark is a compilation of Peter's preaching notes. Though Peter was an Apostle to the Jews (Galatians 2:8), it seems that the intended audience of Mark's Gospel is those with a Roman background. The emphasis in Mark is Jesus' supernatural power and authority – a perspective to which Romans could relate. Mark concentrates on what Jesus did, rather than what He said and taught.

V.   Jude And Hebrews

We are not certain who wrote the letter of Jude. It might have been the Apostle Judas, the son of James (Luke 6:16, Acts 1:13), or it might have been Judas, the Lord's brother (Matthew 13:55).

Jude covers many of the same themes as 2nd Peter. He writes against false teachers and calls on believers to persevere in their faith.

The letter to the Hebrews does not mention the name of the writer. Commentators have made several suggestions, but the majority of ancient writers credit it to Paul.

As its name suggests, Hebrews is intended primarily for Christians from a Jewish background. Like Romans, Hebrews lays out a systematic theology. While Romans describes the theology and process of salvation, the theme of Hebrews is the supremacy of Christ.

1) In Christ there is a superior revelation.

2) Christ is greater than the angels.

3) Christ is the perfect Savior.

4) Jesus is greater than Moses.

5) In Christ we look forward to a greater Sabbath rest.

6) Jesus has a greater priesthood.

7) The New Covenant in Christ is superior to the Old Covenant.

8) Christ's sacrifice is superior to those under the Old Covenant.

9) The hope and faith of the saints of old are realized only in Christ.

Therefore, we can have confidence in God's promises and will receive a kingdom that cannot be shaken if we remain faithful.

VI.   The Ministry Of John

Though John wrote approximately 16% of the New Testament, we know comparatively little about his ministry. Though not mentioned in Acts 15, John apparently was at the Jerusalem Council (Galatians 2:9). This is the last reference to him until Revelation 1, verse 9, which places him on the island of Patmos. How did he get to Patmos, which the Romans used as a penal colony?

From the cross, Jesus entrusted the care of His mother, Mary, to John (John 19:26-28). From then on, John took Mary into his own household. According to tradition, sometime before the destruction of Jerusalem in 70 AD, John moved to Ephesus, taking Mary with him. During one of the persecutions against Christians, John was arrested and exiled to Patmos. After his release, he returned to Ephesus where he died sometime around 100 AD. John was the last of the Apostles to die and the only one to escape martyrdom.

VII.   John's Writings

John wrote his Gospel as a supplement to the other three. He fills in many details which the synoptic Gospels do not record. In addition, John emphasizes the theological importance of the incidents he records. Throughout the book he portrays Jesus as the Son of God.

His stated purpose for writing the book is "...that you may believe that Jesus is the Christ, the Son of God, and that by believing you may have life in his name." (John 20:31 NIV)

In addition to the Gospel, John also wrote three letters. He may have written the first one to counter the philosophy of Gnosticism which was beginning to make inroads in some of the churches. The Gnostics claimed to have special knowledge – that they were the ones who had true spiritual insight and experience. They taught that matter is inherently evil. Therefore, true spirituality is entirely separate from physical action. Since flesh is already evil, there can be no real sins of the flesh.

In his letter, John explores the concept of knowing. How can we know truth? How can we know we are forgiven? How can we know we are in God? John provides a three part answer: Knowledge is based in experience. It results from an obedient and holy lifestyle. And, it is rooted in love. John also provides practical tests by which we can evaluate truth claims.

John's second and third letters are very short. In them he warns against false teachers and emphasizes the necessity of obedience and love.

The last book in the New Testament is the book of Revelation. John wrote it as a result of visions he saw while in exile on the island of Patmos. In many ways Revelation is a counterpart to Genesis. Just as Genesis describes the creation of the universe and the fall of man, Revelation describes the restoration of man and the new heavens to which we look forward. The overall theme of the book is the triumph of Christ over all opposition, and the victory of those who believe in Him.

Application: The purpose of all of the writings of the New Testament is to bring us to faith in Christ, to help us live godly lives as we grow in the knowledge of Christ, and to give us hope and assurance of things to come. Because of the New Testament Scriptures, we can face the future with confidence.

෨෬

Future History

Introduction: The four Gospels teach us about Christ's earthly ministry. The book of Acts gives us insights into the early years of the church and how the Gospel spread through the Roman Empire. We get hints of some of the Apostles' ministry from their epistles. This is past history. But the New Testament also gives us insight about the future. While there are various prophecies in the Gospels and epistles, most of our information about future events comes from the book of Revelation.

For many, the book of Revelation is one of the most puzzling portions of Scripture in the entire Bible. The language and the imagery are so far removed from normal experience that one is tempted to doubt whether he has the capacity to understand it. I suspect that not a few people have wondered whether the majority of the book contains anything to understand, or whether it is merely gibberish. At the same time, Christians are often uneasily aware that the book of Revelation is something which they ought to understand and are plagued by a sense of guilt that they don't.

In the Greek language the title of the book we know as Revelation is "The Apocalypse of John." The word "apocalypse" literally means to uncover or unveil. If the intent of the book is to disclose or reveal what is to come, then we can legitimately ask the question, "Why is it, so often, so obscure and hard for us to understand?" There are at least three answers to this question.

> 1) The first answer lies in the word "apocalypse" itself. It is not only a word which has a meaning, but also describes a type or genre of literature. In other words, the book of Revelation fits into a particular style or class of literature. Unfortunately, it is one with which we are, in general, totally unfamiliar. One of the reasons we find the book hard to understand is that, unlike those in the first century, we don't recognize the conventions of the apocalyptic genre of literature. The imagery and style are foreign to us. We are separated from the book, not only by the time in which we

live and geographical distance from the place where John composed it, but also by our culture.

2) Another reason why the book of Revelation is often hard to understand is because it probably served the same purpose as Jesus' teaching in parables. Jesus taught in parables not only to clearly explain certain principles and concepts to His disciples, but to simultaneously make His teaching obscure to His opponents. Jesus said, "…The knowledge of the kingdom of God has been given to you, but to others I speak in parables, so that, 'though seeing, they may not see; though hearing, they may not understand.'" (Luke 8:10 NIV) At the time the Apostle John penned the book of Revelation, he was in exile for preaching the Gospel. Revelation portrays Christ as the conquering King and the Lord who will overthrow the nations. Further, the book has some harsh things to say about certain powers and/or governments. One reason John wrote the book in the form of an apocalypse may have been to hide the meaning to those in authority while encouraging and giving hope to believers.

3) A third reason the book of Revelation can be hard to understand is that people read it in isolation. But much of the imagery is drawn from other Scripture and, as such, must be interpreted in light of those passages. Similarly, an interpretation of Revelation which does not take into account the definitions which have already been given in other parts of Scripture is unlikely to be accurate.

I.   Four Basic Approaches To Revelation

Through the centuries many people have attempted to interpret Revelation. They have written hundreds of commentaries and preached thousands of sermons on the book. Generally speaking, however, all of the views fall into four broad categories. Though there are many differences, they amount to relatively small details within the major views.

Note: There is a broad consensus that John wrote the first three chapters of Revelation primarily to the seven actual churches in the

Roman province of Asia which he names in the text. Similarly, there is broad agreement that chapters twenty through the end describe the establishment of Christ's Kingdom, the final judgment, and the eternal reward of believers. The four approaches presented below primarily concern the middle sixteen chapters.

1)   The Preterist View

This approach to the book assumes that Revelation describes historical events which have already been fulfilled in, what to us is, the far past. Specifically, it figuratively predicts and describes the events leading up to, and the actual Roman war against the Jewish people which culminated in the destruction of Jerusalem in 70 AD. Some Preterists believe that the entire book has already been fulfilled, while others agree that chapters twenty through twenty-two are yet in the future.

2)   The Historicist View

Historicists view the book of Revelation as a prophecy of the unfolding of history from the time at which John first wrote it until the end of time. In their view, most of the imagery must be taken figuratively. Also, the events of history are, for the most part, revealed in sequential order, though there are some portions of the book which are synchronous (that is occurring at the same time) or in parallel. Some Historicists, particularly those of the Protestant Reformation, also think that the seven churches of Asia mentioned in the first three chapters represent seven eras or epochs of the church.

3)   The Futurist View

With the exception of the first three chapters, Futurists generally believe that the entire book of Revelation has yet to be fulfilled. The middle sixteen chapters predict events which will take place in a short period of time, which Futurists generally think will be three and a half, or seven years in duration. They also tend to interpret the book mostly literally instead of figuratively. In their view, most of the events predicted in Revelation will take place in a linear or sequential manner.

4)   The Idealist or Spiritual View

In the view of Idealists, the visions of Revelation are not tied to any specific historical events at all. The book is almost entirely symbolic, describing spiritual principles and realities in general terms which apply to the church in all ages. They view the various visions as being synchronous, highlighting recurring themes in the battle between good and evil from different perspectives.

II.   Problems With The Four Basic Views

1)   The Preterist View

The Preterist interpretation depends upon John having written the book of Revelation before 70 AD. If John wrote the book at a later date, as many scholars believe, then the Preterist view that Revelation predicts the destruction of Jerusalem cannot be true. In addition, the correlation between the visions and the actual events leading up to the destruction of Jerusalem, is not always obvious and seems somewhat arbitrary.

Those Preterists who believe that the book describes the final return and triumph of Christ as well as the Roman-Jewish wars have a problem similar to the Futurists. They are left with a long historical gap in the narrative. There is a, close to 2,000 year, and growing, gap between the events predicted and Christ's return.

2)   The Historicist View

A serious problem with the Historicist position is that the correlation between the various visions and specific historical events is not always obvious. Interpreters cite comparatively obscure or apparently minor events as fulling the prophecies while ignoring some major events. Also, while there is often a broad consensus among Historicists, they certainly do not always agree on which events fulfill the visions and, especially, in regard to the dates of such periods as the 1,260 days of chapters 11 and 12. When there is so much disagreement, it calls the whole approach into question.

3)   The Futurist View

One of the problems faced by the futurist is that it is impossible to test the interpretation. If the events foretold in Revelation remain in the future, there is no way to tell if one's interpretation of the various visions is accurate. The actual events may prove what Futurists have confidently claimed, to be nothing more than wild speculation with no resemblance to reality.

Another problem Futurists face is that their interpretation necessarily forces a large gap of time between chapter three and the rest of the book. The gap is close to 2,000 years wide now, and can only increase. This does not seem to fit the natural flow of the book.

Those Futurists who believe in a 'pre-tribulation rapture' also face the problem that their interpretation makes the majority of the book of Revelation totally irrelevant for most of the church. If the events described will take place after the church has ascended to heaven, then there seems little point in informing believers what will take place after they have been removed from the scene.

4)   The Idealist View

There is no doubt that God intends all believers throughout the church age to benefit by the book of Revelation. The admonition to 'hear' what is being said is not restricted to the churches which Christ specifically addresses in the first three chapters. (For example, see 1:3 and 13:9). The major problem with the Idealist view is, however, that it does not connect any of the visions to specific historic events. Many see this as a contradiction to the plain or natural meaning of verses such as Revelation 1:1, 1:19, 4:1 and 22:6 which imply a progression of events. Proponents of the other interpretations point out this difficulty by saying that the Idealist view discounts predictive prophecy.

III.   The Millennial Question

Perhaps the most controversial problem in the book of Revelation (some would say the entire Bible) is how to interpret the thousand year reign of Christ mentioned in chapter 20. (Our word millennium comes from the Latin 'mille' meaning thousand and 'annus' meaning years.) Does the thousand years imply an earthly kingdom? When will Christ return in relation to the thousand years? There are three main views:

1)   Premillennial

Premillennialists believe that Christ will return in bodily form and set up an earthly kingdom where He will reign over the nations for a literal thousand years. Some "dispensational" premillennialists hold that this kingdom is distinct from the church. They teach that Christ was unable to establish His Kingdom during His earthly ministry, therefore He instituted the church as a stop-gap measure until Christ is able to set up His Kingdom. Traditional Premilennialism (historically known as Chiliasm), however, sees the Kingdom as a continuation of the church.

The dispensational view is a fairly recent development. In 1830 a Scottish woman named Margaret Macdonald claimed that the Spirit revealed to her that there would be a secret return of Christ before the great tribulation which Revelation 7:14 mentions. At this return, Christ will "rapture" the church. John Darby of the Plymouth Brethren popularized this idea (without attribution). The Scofield Reference Bible and other sources has spread this view even more widely. It is the official position of Dallas Seminary. People such as Hal Lindsay and Josh McDowell have strongly promoted it, as have the Left Behind novels. Going by the radio and TV, one would think that dispensational premillennialism is mainstream. Actually, it is a minority position among scholars. In recent years it has been losing ground against the more traditional premillenial understanding.

2)   Postmillennial

Postmillennialists believe that Christ's second coming will take place after the end of the thousand years. Christ will not reign as an earthly king, but the thousand years will be a time of unprecedented peace and prosperity in which the vast majority of the world's population will live for Christ. After the thousand years, there will be a short time when Satan is loosed and the world will be plunged into wickedness terminating in a final battle. Christ will then return, throw the devil into hell, and judge the world.

3)   Amillennial

Amillennialists believe that the thousand years does not refer to a specific period of time, but rather is simply another way of saying "a very long time." In this view, Christ began to reign when He conquered death by rising from the grave. To put it another way, the Kingdom is in existence now. Christ's church is part of the Kingdom, if not identical with the Kingdom. Christ's death on the cross bound Satan. As in the postmillennialist view, Christ will return after Satan is loosed for a short time.

Note: None of these three views is inseparably tied to any of the four major approaches to Revelation mentioned above. Generally speaking, however, most Futurists tend to take the premillennialist position. Very few Futurists are amillennialists. Similarly, Preterists tend toward the postmillennialist position. Historically, amillennialism has been the most widely held view, particularly among Historicists and Idealists.

IV.   Basic Approach To Interpretation

With this wide range of opinion, what principles should we use to guide our interpretation of the book?

1) Whatever Revelation means, John must have intended for the people to whom he wrote it to understand. Therefore, any interpretation which would have been unintelligible to the Christians in the first century cannot be correct. Similarly, though the message of Revelation has global implications, it seems logical for John to have written it from the geographical perspective of the Roman empire.

2) Our interpretation must be consistent with the genre of literature. Since apocalyptic literature makes heavy use of symbolic language, the majority of the language in Revelation will also be symbolic. We must not interpret symbolic language literally.

3) Our interpretation must harmonize with the rest of Scripture. The meanings John attached to the various symbols and figures in Revelation will most likely be the same as in the passages to which Revelation alludes.

With this in mind, how do I approach the book of Revelation? With humility. Though I have a working hypothesis, I am also aware that I still have much to learn, and may be wrong.

It seems to me that the evidence for a later date of writing is stronger than for an early date. If that is so, it rules out the Preterist position. Also, stopping the 'prophetic clock' for over 2,000 years, as required for the Futurist position, seems totally illogical to me and contrary to the spirit of the rest of Scripture. Therefore, I rule it out.

By upbringing and inclination I am an historicist. There is something very comforting about the notion that God has given us a road-map of future events, and that we can determine where we are in the fulfillment of the divine plan. However, honesty compels me to say that, try as I might, I have been unable to match the visions in Revelation to an actual time-line of history. There are just too many discrepancies between the bold assertions in the commentaries and events as recorded in the history books for me to retain confidence in the Historicist interpretation. The classical understanding that the letters to the seven churches represent seven successive periods in church history is almost certainly wrong. There may be a way to harmonize the prophetic visions in the rest of Revelation with actual history, but I have not found it. Because of these difficulties, I now lean toward the Idealist position. Perhaps the truest understanding of Revelation will come from combining the Idealist with the Historicist approaches. In this combined approach, predictive prophecy is retained without rigidly tying each vision to linear history. I do not claim to have all the answers. There is still much that I do not understand. I am still open to correction and discussion of my basic approach. However, I think I have arrived at an understanding which allows me to move forward.

In regard to the millennial question, I think the amillennial position has the best support from other Scripture. Contra the premillennial position, I think it is pretty clear that Christ is going to return only once – when the dead are raised, just prior to the judgment – and not to establish an earthly kingdom. I also think that there is good evidence that Satan was bound during Christ's first coming. This would rule out the postmillennial understanding that he will be bound just prior to a 1,000 year period sometime in the future. However, I do tend to think that the best days of the church may still be ahead of us. That makes me an optimistic amillennialist!

V.   A Speculative Working Hypothesis

With that background, I offer the following brief synopsis of the book. Please understand that I present it only as a speculative hypothesis. I do not claim that it is right, much less accurate in all particulars. Further research may uncover serious flaws in the basic approach. Nevertheless, I believe that this hypothesis is worth further study.

A key insight to this approach is that Revelation can be divided into seven parallel sections. Each section covers the time period from Christ's ministry to the second coming, but from a different perspective. However, as the book progresses from section to section, the emphasis gradually shifts more from the first coming to the second. In other words, the revelation is progressive as well as synchronous.

1) Chapters 1-3 – Christ is Lord of the Church

The book of Revelation begins with assurance. Whatever may be going on in the world, Jesus loves us! And, He is coming again!

Next is a vision of Christ. He is in control of all of history, past, present and future. He is also Lord of the church.

Then there are letters to seven churches. Christ praises and/or scolds each one according to its spiritual condition. Those who do not repent of sin will be punished. Those who are faithful will be rewarded. Though the letters speak to specific churches, Christ tells everyone to listen to the messages. From this it seems that these seven churches represent churches in every time and place. Regardless of where we happen to be in history, each congregation should evaluate itself by the messages Christ gives to these seven.

2) Chapters 4-7 – The Church in the Midst of Persecution

The second major section of Revelation opens with a vision of heaven's throne room. This vision portrays Christ as a lamb, yet worthy to rule. It is He who controls and unveils the future.

The first six seals which the Lamb opens disclose the socio-economic consequences of obeying the Gospel. Many will be martyred because of the word of God. The time will come, however, when their persecutors will face the wrath of the Lamb.

The section closes with another glimpse of the throne room. This time it is filled with a great multitude of those whom the Lamb has redeemed. Want, persecution and tribulation give way to the redeemed being filled, protected and comforted.

3) Chapters 8-11 – The Church Avenged

The scene now shifts. John wrote the first section from the perspective of how Christ sees the church. The second section highlighted events from the perspective of the church.

Now, in the third section, the vision is of trumpets of warning to those who have oppressed God's people. The warnings include natural disasters, both on land and on sea, spiritual deception, economic disruptions and war.

During this time John measures the church according to a divine standard. In contrast, in spite of all warnings, the world rejects the testimony of the church and attacks it. The church appears destroyed, but God resurrects it. The world then faces judgment, while God's people are rewarded.

4) Chapters 12-14 – The Church vs. Ungodly Government and Philosophy

The fourth section of Revelation covers the same ground as the first three sections, but from the viewpoint of the spiritual struggle which takes place behind the scenes.

Chapter 12 introduces the dragon, a symbol for Satan (Revelation 20:2), and describes his attempts to destroy the church. Chapter 13 depicts two beasts, one from the sea and one from the earth. The sea-beast receives its authority from the dragon, that is, Satan (Revelation 13:2). The sea represents nations (Isaiah 17:12). Therefore, it's likely that the sea-beast represents the satanic power of nations which blaspheme against God by trying to usurp divine authority.

The earth-beast gets its authority from the sea-beast and fully cooperates with it. At the beginning it looks tame, but has great power to do miracles and deceive. Could it be that the land-beast represents earthly wisdom (James 3:14-15), that is science and philosophy, in the service of the state?

Regardless of the identification of the two beasts, the Lamb conquers those who worship the beasts. They are thrown into the winepress of God's wrath when the angels harvest the earth.

5) Chapters 15-16 – Judgment on Impenitent Oppressors

In the fifth section angels pour out the seven bowls of God's wrath. The scene opens in chapter 15 with those who have been victorious over the beast and his image standing beside the sea and singing the song of Moses and the song of the Lamb. The allusion is to the victory song the Israelites sang after God destroyed the Egyptians at the Red Sea (Exodus 15:1-21).

Throughout history it seems like the anti-Christian forces must prevail and overcome the Lord's people. Yet, time after time, it is the oppressor who fails, falls under God's wrath and is destroyed. Chapter 16 ends by describing the total overturning of the established order.

6) Chapters 17-19 – The Church vs. False Religion

Almost all of this section pictures the fall and destruction of an entity which it describes using two different symbols. One of the symbols is a harlot. This woman is a direct contrast to the pure woman of chapter 12. The harlot represents the false church.

The false church also bears the name "Babylon." This is a contrast to the Holy City mentioned in chapter 21.

Both metaphors make it plain that the false church gets along well with the world. It not only caters to the world, it uses the world to gain power and wealth. The false church is also a persecuting power. Whereas the world tries to kill off the true church, it mourns the passing of the false church.

Along with the false church, the false prophet, who was first introduced in chapter 16, is destroyed. The false prophet represents all false religions – specifically those which claim a new or different revelation.

7) Chapters 20-22 – Defeat of Satan and Triumph of the Church

In the last section of Revelation, it is Satan who is overthrown. He is the greatest enemy of the church and the one who motivates and empowers all the other anti-God forces. Christ's first coming – specifically His death, burial and resurrection – greatly curtailed Satan's power. For example, Paul writes, "And having disarmed the powers and authorities, he made a public spectacle of them, triumphing over them by the cross." (Colossians 2:15 NIV).

Before the end, Satan will be let loose for a little while. But this is his last gasp. When Christ returns, Satan will be thrown into hell.

The last two chapters of Revelation depict the destiny of those who have been faithful to Christ. They will live with Christ and God forever. All their hurts and pain will be healed. The nations will reconciled.

V.   A Message Of Hope

Regardless of how one interprets Revelation, we can say with assurance that it is a book of hope. No matter how strong the opposition becomes; no matter how bad the persecution is, the church will be victorious. Christ will judge the nations. His followers will be with Him forever. The curse which came through Adam, will be overturned. The question is: Whose side are we on? Are we ready for Christ's return?

ഇൽൽ

Appendix
Why Revelation? – A Counterpart To Genesis

Aside from alerting believers to future events, what is the purpose of Revelation?

> It is the counterpart to Genesis. Just as Genesis tells how the the universe and mankind began, Revelation foretells the end. The constant theme which runs throughout the Bible is the story of redemption. Genesis relates why we need redemption. Revelation is the culmination of that story. In Revelation there are both similarities to and contrasts with Genesis.

Similarities to Genesis

Genesis	Revelation
1:1 God creates the heavens and the earth	21:1 A new heaven and earth replace the first ones
2:2 God rests from His work	14:13 Those who die in the Lord rest from their labor
2:9 The tree of life is in the garden	22:2 The tree of life is in the New Jerusalem
2:10 A river waters the garden	22:2 A river waters the New Jerusalem
2:16 God gives man freedom to eat of the tree of life	2:7 Christ gives those who overcome the right to eat
	22:14 Rights to tree are given to those who wash their robes
2:19-20 Man names the animals	2:17, 3:12 Christ gives a new name to those who overcome
2:24 Institution of marriage	19:7, 21:2, 21:9 The ultimate expression of marriage

Genesis	Revelation
3:13 The serpent deceives Eve	12:9, 13:14, 20:3, 8, 10 The nations are deceived
3:15 Enmity between the serpent and woman	12:15 The serpent spews water to overtake the woman and sweep her away
3:19 The coming of death	21:8 The second death
3:21 God clothes Adam and Eve	6:11 The martyrs are clothed
6:9 Noah, alone in his generation, walks with God	3:4 A few from Sardis walk with Christ
7:21 All living things not in the Ark perish in water	20:11-15 All who are not in the Book of Life perish in fire
9:13-17 The rainbow is given as a sign of the covenant	10:1 The angel with the scroll has a rainbow above his head
22:1 God tests Abraham	3:10 All on the earth are tested

Contrasts To Genesis

Genesis	Revelation
1:1 God creates the heavens and earth	21:1 The first heavens and earth pass away
2:2 God rests from His work	14:11 There is no rest for those who worship the beast
3:16 Introduction to pain	21:14 There is no more pain
3:17 Creation is cursed	22:3 The curse is removed
3:19 Sweat and toil needed to produce food	7:16 Never again will they hunger
3:19 Death comes	21:4 There is no more death

Genesis	Revelation
3:22-24 Man is forbidden to eat from the Tree of Life	2:7, 22:14 The redeemed are given the right to eat from the Tree of Life
4:7 Cain is mastered by sin	1:5 Those in Christ are freed from sin
6:9 Only Noah is found blameless	14:5 144,000 are found blameless
7:11 Springs of water bring death in the flood	21:6 A spring gives life
10:32 Nations spread out and move away	15:4 Nations come
11:8 The nations are scattered	5:9 Men are purchased from every nation
	7:9 All nations are represented
16:12 Hostility between peoples	22:2 The leaves of the tree are for the healing of the nations

Just as Genesis records mankind's fall and the seeming failure of God's experiment in giving man free will, Revelation records the outcome of mankind's redemption and Christ's triumph over all odds and opposition. Revelation ends with a warning not to tamper with the message. Just as Genesis relates that there was only one way to sin in the Garden of Eden, Revelation emphasizes there is only one way in which we can overcome sin. Eating the forbidden fruit thrust mankind into untold misery. Following Christ will result in bliss beyond the capacity of our imaginations to conceive. Just as Adam and Eve were free to choose sin over obedience, we also are free to choose the water of life. Just as in the Garden of Eden, our eternal destiny hangs on the choice we make.

                                                    ಐಐ

Bibliography

Allen, Roland, *Missionary Methods: St. Paul's or Ours?*, William B. Eerdmans Publishing Company, 1962

Ash, Anthony L. and Cottrell, Jack, Editors, *College Press NIV Commentary*, College Press, various volumes

Cole, Neil, *Organic Leadership: Leading Naturally Right Where You Are*, Baker Books, 2009

Dean, B.S., *An Outline of Bible History*, The Standard Publishing Company, 1912

DOTA (Discipleship Training On The Air), *Revelation*, Programs 369, 374, 379, 381-390

Edersheim, Alfred, *The Life and Times of Jesus the Messiah*, William B. Eerdmans Publishing Company, 1971, 1976

Gaebelein, Frank E., General Editor, *The Expositor's Bible Commentary with the NIV*, Zondervan, various volumes

Gregg, Steve, *Revelation: Four Views: A Parallel Commentary*, Thomas Nelson, 1997, 2013

Maier, Paul L., *Pontius Pilate,* Tyndale House Publishers, Inc., 1968

McBirnie, William Steuart, *The Search for the Twelve Apostles*, Tyndale House Publishers, Inc., 1973

Sandmel, Samuel, *Herod Profile of a Tyrant*, J.B. Lippincott Company, 1967

Whiston, William, Translator, *The Works of Flavius Josephus*, Associated Publishers and Authors Inc.

Wieand, Albert Cassel, *A New Harmony of the Gospels*, William B. Eerdmans Publishing Company, 1950

ಐಓಚ

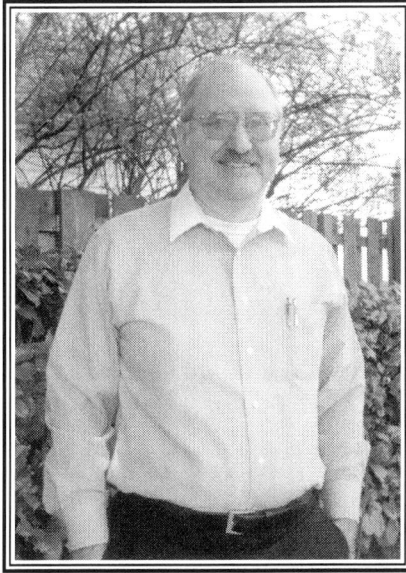

About the Author

Jonathan Turner is both a preacher's kid and a missionary's kid. He grew up in Pakistan where his parents served as church planters. He came to his own faith in Christ through their influence and example.

In addition to writing and teaching, Jonathan is actively involved in carrying on the mission work his parents began. He has also served as an Elder at one of the congregations he attended.

Jonathan and his wife have been happily married for over 30 years. They live in Oregon and have two grown children who are also in the Lord.

You can view some of Jonathan's musings on the church and other aspects of life in Christ at:

www.presbyterjon.com

୫୦୯୫

Made in the USA
Charleston, SC
22 July 2014